The Road to Santiago

Knud Helge Robberstad

THE ROAD TO SANTIAGO

A JOURNEY TO SANTIAGO DE COMPOSTELA

© Knud Helge Robberstad / As Verbum Grafiske
Stavanger, Norway 1996

ISBN 82-994149-1-1

Author: Knud Helge Robberstad
Photography: Knud Helge Robberstad / Mark Baker
Produced by As Verbum Grafiske

Typeset in Futura 9.5 / 13 points of didot.

PROLOGUE

The cathedral is almost deserted. Only a few people in silent prayer are seated on the pews, and the serenity enables us to meditate and pray in peace. We light our candles, and think about those who are important in our lives. The silver coffer with the remains of the Apostle is placed in the crypt. There are no tourists milling around, and I use the opportunity to have a quiet moment to myself. Only James is present. He has been here for a thousand years, I have only just arrived. The silence is all-absorbing, and the experience one of life's magic moments. It is a quarter to seven in the morning. I have just completed my pilgrimage to the shrine of Saint James the Apostle in the Cathedral of Santiago de Compostela.

In the Middle Ages there were hundreds of thousands of people walking to Santiago de Compostela in north-western Spain. They came from all over Europe to seek absolution and the blessing of the Apostle on his grave. Santiago ranked with Jerusalem and Rome as the most important pilgrim sites in the Christian world, and was by far the most popular of these three cities by the 13th century.

The most important pilgrim route went through France, over the Pyrenees westwards through Northern Spain. The route lost some of its importance after the Reformation, but nowadays there are thousands of people travelling along the road to Santiago each year. The means of travel may have changed since the Middle Ages, but the only true pilgrims are those who travel to Santiago on foot, by bike or on horseback.

CONTENTS

Appendices:
Itinerary
Equipment
Bibliography

INTRODUCTION

I became a pilgrim by chance. Initially I was only planning a week's holiday in Spain. I heard about the cathedral in Santiago de Compostela several years ago, and had placed it on my list of places to visit when the opportunity arose.

The cathedral was mainly forgotten until I went to study in Plymouth in Southwest England. Before completing our studies we had to write a dissertation. I was sharing a house with a couple of friends, and we often spent the evenings daydreaming instead of writing. «Have you ever been to Spain?», I asked Mark one evening, the dissertations were so unattractive we both came up with all sorts of excuses to avoid our proof-reading. He had not, so I told him about my travel plans. He liked the idea, and together we started planning a week's trip to the cathedral in Santiago. We intended to catch the ferry from Plymouth to Santander in Northern Spain, and continue by train to Santiago. Little did we know where our plans would eventually lead us.

The dissertations were completed at last, but we did not have the opportunity to go to Santiago at the end of our studies. I went home to Norway, and Mark moved back to London. Every time we discussed a good time to go there was always one of the two main factors lacking; time and money.

At the same time we had expanded our plans a little. Now we wanted to walk to Santiago. I had discovered that the city had been an important pilgrim site in the Middle Ages. Every year thousands of people walked through Europe to visit Saint James's grave at the site of the cathedral. The most important route over the Pyrenees could still be followed across Northern Spain.

The more information we gained about the routes, the longer and more extensive our walk was becoming. If we were to walk from the Pyrenees, why not start from the French side of the mountains, and if we were to walk from France, why not start from one of the starting points of the medieval pilgrims? A pilgrimage in the 20th century, this was becoming exciting!

We decided to set off from the small town of Le Puy-en-Velay in the Massif Central, the central mountain plateau south-west of Lyon. The first recorded pilgrimage to Santiago is Bishop Gottschalk's wandering from Le Puy in year 951. The route he followed is well preserved, and is included as route GR65 in the French network of long distance footpaths, Grande Randonnée. Now, 1,044 years later, we planned to follow in his footsteps as closely as possible.

Ahead of us was a 1,500 kilometre long walk over mountain ranges and plateaus, through dry steppes and green valleys. Such a trip would take considerable preparation, it would not simply be a case of putting on a rucksack and a pair of hiking boots and start walking. The equipment we were to carry would need to cover most of our needs without being too heavy, and physically we needed to be strong enough to be able to walk an average of 30 kilometres per day for 60 days. Strength, stamina and endurance needed careful training, so the body would be able to cope with the strain. I undertook a heavy training programme including jogging, swimming and weight training. Although it was often difficult to find the time or opportunity to carry out this training, my enthusiasm was strong enough to maintain all the blood, sweat and tears.

While I was carrying out my training programme and getting hold of necessary equipment, I obtained as much information about the route and the pilgrimages as possible. During my investigations I came across an organisation in London, The Confraternity of Saint James, founded for the sole purpose of promoting the pilgrim routes and their history. Through this organisation we obtained plenty of useful information. It even produces a special annual pilgrim's guidebook.

Two conditions determined the start of our journey. The Pyrenees had to be crossed when they were free from snow, and the Spanish summer heat was also best avoided. Therefore we had a choice between April and September. The medieval pilgrims usually set off at springtime, in order to be back home again before the winter set in. We had no plans for walking back again, but decided to start walking in the end of April. Then we both had the time and opportunity to accomplish the journey. I took leave from my job in Denmark, and Mark completed the launch of the sailing yacht he was working on before we set out on our walk.

THE LEGEND OF SAINT JAMES

Saint James the Apostle is the patron saint of Spain, and the high protector of the pilgrim road. How he came to be such an important figure for the Catholic church in the Middle Ages is a story spanning several centuries.

James was one of Christ's twelve disciples. He was the son of Zebedee and Salome, brother of John and cousin of Jesus. After the crucifixion of Jesus, James set out to evangelise. He ended up in Spain, and travelled from Andalucia in the south to Galicia in the north trying to convert the pagans. His preaching had little impact until the Virgin Mary appeared before him in Zaragoza. This miracle inspired him to erect the first church dedicated to her. The preaching became more effective when the church was completed.

In the year 44, James returned to Jerusalem. He was accused of heresy, and beheaded by King Herod Agrippa. James thus became the first disciple to be martyred, and one of the very first Christian martyrs. After the beheading his body was thrown to the dogs outside the walls of Jerusalem. The body was rescued by two of his disciples, brought to the port of Jaffa and placed in a boat of marble. The boat had neither crew nor rudder, but an angel steered it across the Mediterranean, through the Strait of Gibraltar and past Portugal to the coast of Galicia. This long voyage miraculously took only seven days. On arrival James was laid on a flat stone, which immediately formed itself into a sarcophagus around his body.

The disciples went to the local king to ask permission to bury the Apostle, but were imprisoned instead. They were later freed by an angel, who came to them in the night and opened the prison door for them to escape. The king's soldiers taking up pursuit were drowned in the foaming waters of a nearby stream when the bridge they crossed collapsed. The king accepted his defeat, and was converted to the new faith. At last James's remains could be given a decent burial. A chapel was built over the tomb, and when the two disciples died they were also placed with the Apostle in his grave.

The grave was forgotten for almost 800 years. In year 813 the hermit Pelagio had a vision; a star was showing the way to the tomb while the sky was filled with celestial music. On the spot the star had illuminated there was found a crypt containing three bodies. Bishop Theodomir from the nearby town of Iria Flavia declared these to be the remains of James and his two disciples. A small church was built over the grave, and a monastery for an abbot and twelve monks built nearby. The town which grew up around the monastery became known as Campo de la Estella; the Field of the Star. James was called Santo Iago in old Spanish. Thus the name Santiago de Compostela; Saint James of the Field of the Star.

King Alfonso II of Asturia and León proclaimed James to be the patron saint of Christian Spain. This would come in useful when the Islamic Moors were to be expelled from the country. In the Battle of Clavijo, fought in year 844, the Saint was on the Christian side. With his sword held high aloft he came riding out of the sky on his white charger, and beheaded 50,000 Moors during the battle. Hence he became known as Santiago Matamoros; Saint James the Moor-slayer. Loyalty and devotion to him was forever linked to the Christian battle against the Infidel. Between the 9th and the 17th centuries he appeared in almost forty battles. His appearance in all these battles marks a sharp contrast to his preaching about loving your neighbour as yourself.

James was depicted as saint, warrior and pilgrim. The pilgrim's hat and staff became his insignias. His saints-day is celebrated on the 25th July, to commemorate the day on which he is said to have been buried in Compostela. When this day falls on a Sunday the year is known as Año Santo, a Holy Year. 1993 was the last holy year, 1999 will be the next. In a holy year the number of pilgrims is at its highest.

Originally the pilgrims walked to the Apostle's grave to do penance and show their gratitude. During the centuries this grew into the cult of Saint James, and the number of pilgrims involved made it necessary to develop the infrastructure along the various routes. The worshipping of James was especially stimulated by the Benedictine monastery of Cluny in France. The Cluny monastery had a major influence over the pilgrim roads, building churches, monasteries, bridges and hostels all along the route to take care of the pilgrims spiritual and physical needs.

THE ROAD TO LE PUY

We met up in Paris before continuing to Le Puy. Paris might not be a city usually associated with pilgrims, but in the Middle Ages the city was actually the starting point of one of the largest religious migrations in the history of Europe. In the 11th century, almost half a million people travelled annually along the various pilgrim routes through France. Most pilgrims from the northern parts of Europe passed through Paris.

The starting point was the church of Saint Jacques-de-la-Boucherie on Place Saint Jacques near the cathedral of Notre-Dame. The church was originally dedicated to Saint Martin, but he was rapidly replaced by Saint James, Jacques in French, since a change of name was expected to increase the church's popularity and income. The belfry is all that now remains, the rest of the church was demolished during the French Revolution. At the base of the belfry the word «zero» is inscribed to show that this is the beginning of the road to Santiago. The pilgrim route at the church-steps continued past Notre-Dame, across the Seine along the Rue Saint Jacques and out of Paris.

Outside Notre-Dame stands a bronze statue of Emperor Charlemagne and his knights Roland and Oliver. The song about Roland's death in the Pyrenees was the pilgrims' favourite epic. It was written around year 1100, and describes Christian France's struggle against the pagan Saracens in Spain. In the late Middle Ages it was recited by troubadours along the road to give the pilgrims strength and courage to continue on the road to Compostela.

Roland is the hero of the poem. With his sword, Durandal, he fought the infidels after Charlemagne had invaded north-eastern Spain and knocked down the walls surrounding the old Basque capital of Pamplona. When Charlemagne withdrew his army to France, the Basques took their revenge. In a wooded pass near Roncesvalles in the Pyrenees, they attacked the rearguard in an ambush. The rearguard was commanded by Roland, and only when the numbers of the opposing forces became too many did he sound his ivory horn, Oliphant, to summon aid from the Emperor's army. It is said that on his third desperate blast he blew so hard that the horn broke, the ground shivered and the birds fell down from the trees. The Emperor heard the sound on the other side of the mountains, and returned to their rescue. It was too late, the Basques had almost annihilated the entire rearguard. Roland and Oliver were both killed in the Battle of Roncesvalles.

The poem claims that the rearguard was attacked by the Saracens, but this was possibly a rewriting of the truth in order to make Roland's death more heroic. The Santiago legend tells how James was a source of inspiration and encouragement to Charlemagne during his delivery of Spain. Charlemagne is also claimed to be the first pilgrim to Santiago.

Back in Rue Saint Jacques there now remains very little to show that this was once an important pilgrims' way, apart from a couple of eroded scallop shells on the walls and the fact that it is the address for several sports dealers' selling camping equipment, hiking boots and blister remedies. We were going to follow the route used during the first pilgrimage, and caught a train from Paris to Le Puy in the Massif Central.

It took us the whole day to get to Le Puy, as we had to

The Cathedral of Notre-Dame in Le Puy.

change trains a couple of times and catch a bus for the final stretch. The bus took us through a rolling countryside of valleys and green hills. Grey-brown houses with orange-tiled roofs are grouped into villages clinging to the hillsides, as they have done since before medieval times.

At last we spotted Le Puy in the distance. It is a charming town of 26,000 citizens. The town is built around a *puy*; a pyramid-shaped volcanic rock jutting out from the even landscape. The streets in the old town are narrow, steep and twisted, and the cobblestones are laid so unevenly that riding a bicycle in the old quarters is not recommended for anyone with false teeth.

On top of the cliff sits a rust-red statue of Notre-Dame-de-France. This 16 metre high statue of the Virgin and Child was made of metal from canons captured by the French during the Crimean War. Through the peeping holes in the top of the statue we got a superb view of Le Puy and the terrain we would be walking through during the first stretch of the road to Santiago.

Below the statue is the cathedral of Notre-Dame-du-Puy. It has been built on several levels to blend into the steep rock face, and seems to be resting on the long flight of steps leading up to the main portal. The main entrance is situated underneath the choir, so we had to walk upstairs to get into the nave.

Le Puy has always been a sacred place. The steep cliffs were used as places of worship long before Christianity came to France. An Egyptian statue of the Virgin Mary established the town as a pilgrim centre. This statue was also destroyed during the French Revolution, but visitors arriving at the 900 years old cathedral today will instead see a small statue of the Black Virgin.

We walked up the steep streets to visit the cathedral and to sign our names in the pilgrim book housed in the sacristy. The sacristy also functions as a souvenir shop, and was packed with French tourists looking for appropriate souvenirs. The tiny lady behind the counter got very ex-

The volcanic rocks have given Le Puy its name.

Le Puy is a picturesque town with narrow streets.

cited when I showed her our pilgrim's records. I asked her politely in my very simple French if we could have them stamped. A pilgrim's record is issued by The Confraternity of Saint James to members who are following the road to Santiago. The record should be stamped in churches, monasteries, town halls or bars along the road. On our arrival in the cathedral in Santiago it would qualify us to receive the Compostela; the certificate proving that we had completed our pilgrimage. The Compostela is dated back to the 14th century, and offers the pilgrim absolution and halves his time in purgatory. In the sacristy in Le Puy the stamp is locked away in an old wooden cabinet. The cabinet is hanging above a long bench along the wall, and the tiny lady had to stand on her tiptoes and use a wooden ruler to reach it. We received our first stamps, and were now officially registered as pilgrims on the way to James's grave.

One further important detail remained before we could set out on our walk; acquiring a Coquille Saint Jacques, the scallop shell which is the very symbol of the Jacobean pilgrims. The scallop shell is a symbol several thousand years old, and is probably of Hellenistic origin. Venus, the goddess of love, was born in a scallop shell, and the shell was therefore used as a symbol of love. It has been the pilgrim insignia since before the 11th century, and was probably adopted to distinguish pilgrims from other travellers. The shell was usually carried on the hat or coat, and later buried with the pilgrim in his grave. It was often used as an insignia in the crest of the returned pilgrim.

The oldest legend of the scallop shell tells of how the Apostle used the shell when baptising new Christians in Spain. Another legend tells of how a young Spanish nobleman fell into the sea, drowned and was brought back to life by James, who emerged from the water with scallop shells clinging to his robe.

Le Puy is a considerable distance from the coast, and the only place where shells can be obtained is at a goldsmith's shop. He ground them into a practical size for our use, and Madame got hold of some leather straps to fasten the shells to our rucksacks. Now we had everything ready for our journey along the pilgrim road to Santiago.

The statue of Notre-Dame-de-France.

THE ROAD FROM LE PUY TO CONQUES

We began our journey from Le Puy on a rainy morning at the end of April. The walking route GR65 starts from the square Place du Plot, where a statue of James watches over those who start walking the route to his grave. It was Sunday, and the normally busy market square was lying deserted and quiet. Rue Saint Jacques and Rue de Compostelle led us out of town through the old quarters.

The route was easy to follow. The French Rambler's Association has marked it with its characteristic red and white horizontal flashes. Where the lines crossed we were on the wrong path. In addition we were carrying a French guidebook with the route clearly drawn on 1:50,000 scale maps. The old pilgrim routes were marked with crosses, and several of them are still visible along the road.

Le Puy lies at just over 625 metres above sea level, and the route took us swiftly up to 1200 metres along a combination of tarred roads, cart tracks, paths and gullies. The temperature was pleasantly mild, and we found it more convenient to wear shorts. In case of showers, bare legs would dry quicker than a pair of long trousers, and shorts were also easier to clean.

We tried to keep a slow pace, and not be too eager on this first day, otherwise we would regret it tomorrow. We stopped wherever convenient along the route to admire the view, or to have something to eat.

Our guidebook mentioned that the dogs along this first stretch were especially irritating. We did not experience any problems with them on that day. One must expect some barking when passing through farmyards, but the dogs were generally too cowardly to approach us.

A white bitch of unknown breed even kept us company for a while. She stared, almost longingly, after us when we left her to follow the marked route across some open fields.

The first week would be hard, both physically and mentally. We had to get used to walking the daily stretches and establish a daily routine that would become an essential part of our lives for the next two months or so to come. Our bodies had to get used to the weight of our backpacks, and our legs had to adjust to the combination of distance and weight. All our equipment had been tried out and broken in beforehand, so we knew everything was in order, but now it all had to work simultaneously for the first time. In addition we were in unknown territory in a country where we hardly spoke the language, and practical details such as food and accommodation had to be sorted out along the way.

In France there is a well-developed system of *Gîtes d'etape*; hostels for walkers. The standard varies considerably, but at least you get a roof over your head for a reasonable price. We were planning to sleep in *gîtes* whenever possible, and, as pilgrim, we also had the opportunity of staying in some of the monasteries along the route.

The terrain was relatively flat when we reached the higher altitude. The road zigzagged across the mountain plateau, past fields and hamlets, through a mixture of deciduous and coniferous forests. We met two middle-aged French walkers, who kept us company for a while until our pace became too fast for them. Most of the

The GR65 is marked with red and white flashes.

Landscape from the Massif Central towards La Rode.

Waymark along the pilgrim route.

villages were down in the valleys, so we sometimes had to do a bit of climbing. All the ascents and descents were hard on the legs, and we were pretty exhausted when we finally arrived at the *gîte* in Monistrol-d'Allier on our first evening. Moreover, both of us had developed blisters! They were not large or serious, but had to be treated properly to avoid infections and other problems.

The *gîte* in Monistrol had two small dormitories, a simple kitchen, two showers and toilets of the «hole-in-the-floor» variety. During the evening we were joined by several other walkers, amongst them the two French gentlemen. Most of the others were only going to follow sections of the Chemin Saint Jacques; the French Road to Santiago. Whilst washing our clothes I got to chat with a Dutch lady. She had previously walked various parts of the route, but had never been to Santiago. Her dream was to walk all the way from the Netherlands to Santiago. She believed it would take about five months to complete such a walk.

Before going to bed we massaged our feet and stretched our leg muscles, in order to be ready for a new stretch of road tomorrow. We were sharing the dormitory with the two French gentlemen, and slept like logs, despite the mattress springs squeaking with every movement.

A day starts early when staying with other walkers. We let the others set off first, and started our day by buying fresh pastry for breakfast from a tiny *pâtisserie*. The small village church was locked, but Madame in the *pâtisserie* determinedly took out her stamp when I asked her where we could get our pilgrim's records stamped. The records should have been stamped by the local vicar, but Madame both signed and dated the stamps. She had obviously done it before.

From Monistrol we continued up a steep and winding hill. The sky was grey, and a change of weather could have been to the better or worse. Our feet were sore from yesterday's walking, so we were moving forwards rather slowly. Almost at the top of the hill we stopped by a cast-iron cross to admire the view over the river Allier. The sun was breaking through the morning mist, and we ate our breakfast overlooking the village and river below us. Freshly baked *croissants* taste incredible when eaten outdoors.

The road continued uphill, and we passed through a hamlet with a selection of dogs in all shapes and sizes. They were fairly noisy, but kept a safe distance from us.

The route shifted between tarred country lanes and grassy cart tracks. The grassy surface was a blessing for sore feet. When the pain became too much we stopped for lunch on a hillside. We had bought fresh *baguettes* that morning, and I had packed mine under the top lid of my rucksack. Not a clever thing to do, as the *baguette* had been squeezed into the shape of pitta bread. I did, however, manage to push in a small piece of Camembert and some salami. Together with fresh spring water it made a tasty lunch. A couple of eagles were circling high above the road hunting for mice and other rodents, and life really was not too bad.

As soon as we were back on tarred road again the pain in my feet increased, caused by the sole of the foot being pressed against the hard surface. Our progress was slow, with many stops to drink water or catch our breath. The terrain was fortunately not as steep any more, but the sun was warming from an almost cloudless sky. Both of us were limping, and Mark had lost the feeling in his toes and large parts of the soles of his feet. The insoles of his boots were not absorbing the impact, so he took them out in hope that it would get better. I had brought a pair of spare soles, and cut them down to his shoe size. They helped a little, but it was going to take nine weeks before he got any feeling back in his feet again.

It was obvious that we had walked further than we should have that day, but we were in the middle of nowhere, and the nearest *gîte* was still some distance away. We had to continue. I checked our map and guidebook to try to find somewhere closer to stay, but to no avail. It was tempting to catch a lift on one of the tractors driving past. What would a medieval pilgrim with sore feet have done?

On the outskirts of Le Villeret d'Apchier stood a small sign pointing towards the village café. Someone had quite recently added *chambre* and *duche*; room and shower. Our prayers may well have been heard. We agreed to investigate the matter further, and tried to ask for directions in the village, but just when our French did not seem to be producing any results, an old English-speaking gentleman came to our rescue. He took us down to the café outside

The road ahead from La Roche.

Madame Julien's house, and explained our business to the hostess.

We soon found ourselves at a picnic table on Madame's terrace, where she served us refreshments of a kind that made us forget our sore feet. She offered us the use of the family's refurbished woodshed for the night, and her daughter immediately started making the room ready. After having inspected the premises we decided it was perfect. We showered, plastered our feet and made ourselves presentable before limping into Madame's conservatory. Here she dished up a five-course meal of supreme quality. The portions were very generous, so we must have looked pretty hungry and exhausted.

After the meal we had a long chat with Monsieur Julien on the terrace. The conversation was in a mixture of French, English and body language, and he explained that most people estimated the stretch from Le Puy to Le Villeret to be a three-day walk. We had only used two days to cover this distance, which might explain why we were a little stiff and footsore.

Next morning we got ready for Madame Julien's *petit dejeuner;* breakfast, which was not much less superior from yesterday's evening meal. The coffee was served in bowls, as is the French custom, and Madame offered freshly made *croissants,* scones and home-made jam. I felt in much better shape after a good night's sleep, and the conversation around the table was rather lively. Most of the 50 inhabitants in the village made their living from agriculture and sheep, and Madame's only opportunity to make a few francs on the side was to run a café for walkers during the summer season. Her four daughters had all moved away from home, the youngest was only home on vacation from the university in Nice where she was studying medicine.

Madame Julien offered to make a reservation for us at Madame Jalbert's in La Roche, a tiny village about 12 kilometres further along the road. A short distance was just what we needed that day, and we accepted her offer gratefully. Monsieur Julien weighed our rucksacks on a fish scale before we left. Mark's weighed almost 30 kilos! Mine was a little lighter. The camera equipment accounted for most of the weight, but we decided to go through our packs more thoroughly and send off everything that was not absolutely necessary. We said goodbye to the Juliens, and promised to send them a postcard from the City of the Apostle before wandering off to new adventures.

We walked at a moderate pace along the road to La Roche and Madame Jalbert's residence. Every time we stopped we both kept the conversation going to delay the departure as long as possible. On the rocks along the path we saw lizards dozing in the sun, and when reaching a spring protected by a statue of Saint Roch, we quenched our thirst before following the lizards' example.

Saint Roch is one of the many saints protecting pilgrims along the road to Santiago. He was born in France in the middle of the 13th century, and spent much of his life on pilgrimages. In Italy he caught the plague, and to avoid infecting others he settled down in the woods. He was soon reputed to have cured other sufferers from the plague, and when he died several miracles were claimed to have occurred on his grave. A small dog brought him food when he was in the woods, and along the pilgrim road he is often pictured with a wound on his leg, accompanied by a small dog with a loaf of bread in its mouth.

Madame Jalbert had just finished her shopping at the local mobile supermarket when we arrived at her house. She is a tall, muscular and strong-willed lady in her sixties, of the kind not to be argued with. After we had drunk several cups of strong coffee in her kitchen she showed us to our room on the third floor. Being her only guests we got what was almost like a small flat at our disposal.

Madame only spoke French, but by using the dictionary and a notepad we managed to understand each other. Even the simplest subjects are complicated when trying to use a language you are not familiar with, and after a long time we finally found out when Madame had said she would have the evening meal ready. Even if the conversation was a bit limited, we enjoyed our stay at Madame Jalbert's.

She showed us a copy of an article from the American Gourmet Magazine. The journalist Herb McGrew had visited the Massif Central in search of the local cuisine, and had paid a visit to Madame Jalbert. In the article he praised her food, and, after a superb five-course meal, we could only agree with his conclusion, that the more humble the restaurant, the nobler the food. We took notes of other places mentioned in his article, and the following week we combined our pilgrimage with a journey through French gastronomy.

The sun shone from a cloudless sky and the weather forecast predicted a temperature of around 23°C when we left Madame Jalbert the following morning. The blisters were properly plastered, but I was a little worried about a blister on the inside of my ankle. It did not seem to be getting any better, and the fluid content seemed to be increasing from day to day.

The road took us through pine forests and along green fields full of dandelions, and we were once again 1200 metres up. Our packs were thoroughly checked the night before, and we planned to stop at the post office in Saint-Alban-sur-Limagnole to post home articles that were not absolutely necessary.

On arrival in Saint-Alban we greeted everyone we met with our usual *bonjour*. The response here was minimal, and the empty looks we received may have been explained by the fact that the village hospital was some kind of a mental institution. We found the post office after some searching, and by pointing in a brochure we acquired boxes for the dispatch. The lady behind the counter seemed to understand our requirement when I explained that we wanted to send the parcels *non-rapide* for a *petit prix!*

New provisions had to be bought, and Mark walked over to the butcher's to buy some salami. After several attempts at trying to explain in French that he wanted to taste a *petit* slice, and being shown sausages of different sizes, but none of trial-size, he finally gave in and accepted the last sausage the butcher pointed at. My task in Madame's grocery shop was a little easier.

Equipped with a fresh loaf of bread and several other necessary groceries we continued our journey. The temperature was at its peak, so we stopped somewhere in the shade for our lunch. I felt a little faint, but believed some food would improve my condition.

When walking up a steep climb through the forest I realised that I was not feeling at all well. I tried to tell Mark, who was walking in front, but my lips had dried to my teeth so I had to loosen them with my fingers before I could pronounce any words. I was becoming dehydrated. Mark immediately ordered a halt. He made me strip to the waist to cool down, and lie down with my feet high to increase the blood circulation to my head. He gave me some water to moisten my lips, and we shared the last of the chocolate and some sugared water to boost our energy level. Slowly, but surely, the energy returned. When I had recovered sufficiently to entertain him with stories from the green pastures of my childhood it was time to continue.

A long and painful descent led us to the village of Les Estrets, where, according to our guidebook, we would find somewhere to spend the night. We did not find anywhere, and decided to continue over the next hill. We were almost forced aside from the village's only water fountain by an old lady dressed in black. She was very impatient to get her water containers filled, and showed little regard for thirsty pilgrims.

The route involved another climb along a woodland road with deep wheel tracks in the sandy ground. I had now passed the pain barrier, and continued solely on my willpower and my instinct of self-preservation. I do not remember much of the landscape, but kept myself engaged by mentally going through the contents of my rucksack and what was absolutely necessary for the rest of the journey. Do I need a sleeping bag in this heat? The small travelling towel could be cut in half, the soap bar could definitely be cut in half. Do we really need a tube of toothpaste and a deodorant each? Everything we cut down on would reduce the weight, even if we initially set off with what we thought was very little equipment. My train of thought may not have been highly rational, but it was literally keeping me going.

The final stretch of that leg was pure suffering, but it never crossed my mind to give up, or to cancel the next part of the journey. During the time it took us to walk to Santiago I only had two days when I had to tell myself that every single step was bringing me one step closer to my goal. This was one of them.

At long last we got to the *gîte* in Aumont-Aubrac, that day's destination. Both of us were exhausted, and we needed several refreshments in the café upstairs before feeling energetic enough to walk around the corner and move into the *gîte* below. It was almost a divine sensation having a shower after a long and hard day. We stretched our tender muscles and took a look at our blisters. They

The church of Saint Etienne where we lit candles for sore feet.

had worsened considerably. Mark's soles were blood-stained and looked terrible, and the blister on my ankle had gone deep purple and grown to the size of a golf ball. It was filled with fluid, and the whole ankle was swollen. Something had to be done, but we decided to wait until the next day to see what developed.

We gave ourselves a rest-day in Aumont-Aubrac to recover and regain our strength. The next morning we limped to the village *pharmacie* to get professional aid. I removed my sock and shoe to show off the problem, and was immediately surrounded by five formidable French Madammes who began ah-ing and oh-ing. I was told that a visit to Monsieur le Docteur up the road was advisable. We limped up the road, luckily it was not too far, and I was led into the doctor's study at once.

Monsieur le Docteur was a well-dressed gentleman,

and when, with difficulty, I had managed to get onto the bench he began his examination. He talked a lot in French, even though I had explained that I did not speak the language, and used a syringe to suck up as much fluid as possible. Then he filled the blister with iodine to prevent infection, before he looked earnestly at me over the rim of his glasses. «No marche deux jour» needed no translation; I had been banned from walking for two days!

There was not much else to do but follow the doctor's orders, so we limped back to the *gîte* after stopping in the church of Saint Etienne to light candles for sore feet. We spent the rest of the day checking our packs, washing all our clothes and getting them properly dry. In previous days we had not been able to dry our clothes properly, and even though they dried quite rapidly on our bodies, it did not compare with drying in the sun. They also smelt fresher that way.

In the afternoon we met the first fellow members of The Confraternity of Saint James. Serena and Richard, a couple of English nurses in their late twenties, had taken leave from their work at a hospital in Southampton to walk to Santiago. Allan, an Englishman in his early sixties, had just retired from a position as Marine Director of Hong Kong Waters. He wanted to spend the time along the road to Santiago contemplating how to spend his retirement. The modern pilgrim often stands at a crossroads in his life, and needs time to go through the alternatives before making up his mind.

The other three had set off from Le Puy the day after us. We exchanged experiences from the route so far, and discussed, amongst other things, what we could do to further reduce the weight of our rucksacks. A Dutch couple in their forties arrived in the afternoon, and we all spent the afternoon and evening engaged in lively chatter. This might have been linked to the fact that we began the evening drinking beer in the restaurant upstairs before moving on to the meal accompanied by wine. In any case it made for a very pleasant evening with lots of laughter, despite the blisters and the stiffness.

The following day we cheated! After two nights in Aumont-Aubrac it was time to move on, so we got a taxi to take us the 26 kilometres to Nasbinals. The countryside was beautiful with bare ridges, dry-stone walls and mountain farms scattered around, 1200 metres above sea level. It re-minded me of Dartmoor in Southwest England, with few chances of finding shade. I did not envy those who had to walk over the moors in the heat, and we did not have guilty consciences for having used modern means of transport. A medieval pilgrim would more than likely have accepted a lift on a hay cart if he was given the opportunity. There is a difference between being sensible and being stubborn, and every solution has to be based on the facts of the situation.

We arrived in Nasbinals in the morning, and settled down on a bench outside the church. Nasbinals is a small village with the standard contents; a church, a war memorial, two small hotels, four bars, a tourist office, a few shops and a water fountain. I kept an eye on our rucksacks while Mark went for a stroll around the village, that only took three minutes.

A wooden sculpture of James is placed on a shelf in a corner of the church. He is dressed like a pilgrim, with a hat, a staff and a scallop shell. Two versions of the Virgin Mary are standing in the side chapels. The artists have obviously had different views upon how the Holy Lady might have looked; one is tall and skinny with an unproportional head, the other a more chubby version.

The sun was scorching here at 1300 metres altitude. Fortunately, the felt hats we bought from the hatter's in Saint James's Street in London provided good protection against the sun. It seemed a little odd to be carrying gloves and woolly hats in the heat wave we were experiencing, but we would possibly encounter snow and frost before crossing the Pyrenees. Later we received information that there was a heavy snowfall the week after we crossed the Massif Central, so we had not miscalculated the seasons completely.

Allan walked by in the afternoon. He had experienced a long and hot day, and even if he had planned to walk on, he did not need much encouragement to stop. The *gîte* did not open until five, and the three of us were the only guests. We were accommodated in the attic in a long dormitory with room for fifteen people. The standard was good and the hostess friendly. However, no one had so far excelled Madame Julien and her woodshed.

After supper there was nothing else to do but go to bed. Bedtime around nine-thirty was fairly uncommon for us, but we were planning an early start the next day, and so needed all the sleep we could get.

War memorial in Nasbinals.

During the night it got a little chilly. I had to put a quilt over the woollen blanket in order to keep warm. The sleeping bags were only used the first night, then they proved too hot. Since then a woollen blanket over the thin silk liners had been enough to keep us warm.

The following day we took it easy in order to give our feet a chance to recover. We were to have problems with our feet throughout the French part of the journey, but never as severe as during the first week. We expected it to be hard in the beginning, but had not expected the problems to be quite so serious. It was a barrier we had to break through.

The road from Nasbinals went through a beech forest in full leaf, before reaching the barren hills again. The countryside is open grassland, with the odd tree and stone walls following the contours of the rolling hills. Some old farms and hay barns lie scattered around.

The morning light was magnificent, and we made several halts to photograph the beautiful scenery and the snow-capped mountains to the north. We placed a bet with Allan for a bottle of wine the night before that it really was snow we had seen on the peaks. He was convinced it was only limestone. Here we were gathering photographic evidence that we were right.

When trekking one tends to greet everybody one meets. It gave us the opportunity to speak a little French, and we often stopped for a chat with the people we met. The subjects were simple topics like the weather, where we were from and where we were heading. This became somewhat of a problem when we suddenly encountered an off-road bicycle race in the middle of the moors, and were almost run down by nearly two hundred cyclists coming towards us. There was only time for a quick *bonjour* to every cyclist before they moved on, but our French seemed to slowly improve with the passing of the race.

Landscape from the Massif Central.

The snow-capped mountains in the Auvergne later brought us a bottle of wine.

View from the highest point along the French Road.

Luxuriant scenery from the lowlands towards Saint Come-d'Olt.

The road cuts through deep valleys towards Saint-Chely-d'Aubrac.

That day's stage took us to the highest point on the French road. From this hill, 1360 metres above sea level, we could see the village of Aubrac with its towers and turrets below us. The village was founded in year 1120 by the Flemish knight Adalard. He crossed the plateau in a furious blizzard on his way to Santiago, and in gratitude for having survived the storm he built a hostel here as a place of refuge for other pilgrims. The village looked rather interesting from a distance, but after visiting the monastic church and scaring off all the ravens we made a rapid decision to continue. Aubrac consists of four hotels that probably had their heydays before the 1930's. Today the village seems most suitable for movies á la Psycho.

From Aubrac the road descends through beech forests and across open fields down towards an altitude of 800 metres. The Massif Central is one of the poorest regions in France. The farms are remotely located, and the run-down buildings are a clear indication of the fact that the elders are left in the country while the young have left to seek employment in the towns. In several villages we only saw old people, no children playing outside the houses, and much of the land lies fallow. The churches also bear marks of decay, and although they were always open for us to light our candles of reflection, it was obvious that for several years maintenance had been kept to a minimum.

The sun shone from a deep blue sky and the thermometer showed a temperature of 29°C as we left the Massif Central Plateau. During the following three weeks we would be walking through a terrain which is 75 to 500 metres above sea level.

The river Lot runs lazy and wide through green valleys westwards to Bordeaux and the Atlantic Coast. We crossed it for the first time at Saint-Come-d'Olt, and would be crossing it again several times over the next few weeks.

Our guidebook recommended a visit to the small church of Saint-Pierre in Bessuéjouls. The church is

The river Lot runs lazily through Espalion.

The church of Saint-Pierre in Bessuéjouls is well worth a visit.

remotely located near the Lot, and the interior of the nave is plain with no decorations. A narrow stone stairway leads up into the tower, where a small chapel with sandstone columns and arches can be found. The chapel was built in the 11th century, and the columns are richly ornamented. Amongst archangels and knot patterns there are carvings of female figures. The way they are posed indicates that they are not meant to symbolise any Holy Virgin, they are probably of a more pagan origin…

Mark began experiencing problems with his Achilles tendons, so we decided to follow the even road along the Lot rather than the steep GR65 over the hills. An adder slithered across the road ahead of us, and disappeared rapidly into a whole in the roadside. Lizards were seen regularly, and along the narrow paths we could hear them scurrying through the grass to take cover.

A long narrow bridge took us across the Lot to Estaing. This picturesque little town is built around a hill with a high, pointed castle on top. We stopped at the first bar to get the key to the *gîte*, which is located in a disused medieval chapel. The nave is partitioned by an extra floor, a dormitory has been built over the altar and a kitchen, showers and toilets have been fitted into the entrance hall.

Outside the church of Saint Fleuret we met a nun dressed in a blue habit. I showed her our pilgrim's records, and she invited us into the sacristy to have them stamped. It was a rather special experience following her into the church and watching her perform the sign of the cross, curtseying and praying in several directions. When one has not been raised as a Catholic the whole ritual is rather unknown, and we felt pretty hopeless while discreetly trying to copy some of her movements.

The convent is located in the castle across the square from the church, and the view from its tower over the town and the river is said to be stunning. We explained to the Sister that we would like to visit the convent. Like the true pilgrims we were, she guided us through the convent gate, through the outer courtyard and up into the inner one to present us to the Mother Superior. The Mother gave us a stern look, and told us to mind our heads in the narrow stairwell before allowing us up into the tower. The view

Newly ploughed fields along the river Lot.

was worth the hassle, we got a panoramic view of Estaing, the Lot and the surrounding hills.

It was getting close to vespers, the nuns' evensong, so we thought it best to leave the convent. We were taken to the gate by a smiling nun, who locked the gate firmly behind us. The visit to the convent had caused us a minor problem; how do you address a nun? She is not Madame nor Mademoiselle. Next time we would try *soeur;* Sister, to see if that was accepted.

Back in our little chapel we were half expecting to be woken during the night by some jocular saint, but as pilgrims we slept safely under the protection of the Apostle.

After the first hard week we had developed a daily routine that worked. We woke up at five-thirty to be ready for departure around seven at break of dawn. Breakfast normally consisted of a calorie-rich and nutritious combination of biscuits, cakes, yoghurt, water and fruit juice, and we usually bought fresh *croissants* and *baguettes* from *pâtisseries* along the route. To avoid the midday heat we tried to walk as far as possible before stopping for lunch. The daily distances were getting longer, and although we were still having problems with our feet, it was nothing compared to what we suffered during those first couple of days.

We spent most of the day along the road, stopping whenever we decided to visit churches and other places of interest. We were never in a rush to get to our next

Estaing Castle.

View over Lot and Estaing.

Interior in the church of Saint Fleuret.

Stained-glass window in Estaing.

Landscapes along the road to Conques.

overnight stop, and it was often late in the afternoon before we reached our destination. Our first port of call was always a refreshment stop; cold beer and coffee in the nearest bar, before moving into the *gîte*.

The afternoons were spent planning the next day, writing our journals, talking to fellow walkers and washing our clothes. We had only brought one spare set of underwear, T-shirts and socks each. Therefore afternoons were also spent changing and washing our dirty clothes in order to have clean clothes for the following afternoon. This system worked fine during the entire walk.

New provisions had to be bought every day, so we did not have to carry too much food. We always had a small emergency supply of fruit and chocolate tucked away, and a small salami, a Camembert and some tomatoes were always available for lunch. Drinking water was not a problem. The water bottles were filled in the *gîte* every morning, and 1.5 litres was generally enough for a whole day.

Food was essential for our well-being, and our only luxury was eating out every night. Most *gîtes* had cooking facilities, but it was worth eating in restaurants and cafés rather than cooking ourselves. A five-course meal, including wine and bread, costs between 50 to 70 francs, 6 to 9 pounds, and therefore not that extravagant. We were often served local specialities and dishes made from old family recipes. Naturally the menus were presented in French, and we usually ordered the dishes with the most interesting names. Therefore we rarely knew what we had ordered until the dishes were brought in. Eating out became more exciting this way, although one week we ended up eating lamb chops five days in a row!

We left the river Lot to walk across the hills towards Conques a bit further south. I had sent off depot-parcels to several post offices along the route. The parcels contained new films, a map book and information about the next section of the route. In addition I had organised them so that we could use the packing to send off exposed films, used maps and other superfluous articles.

Our first depot stop was in Conques. The town is beautifully located on a luxuriant hillside by the river Dourdou. The cathedral of Sainte Foy is one of the five most important cathedrals along the pilgrim way. Its interior is light and bright despite being Romanesque, and when the church was filled with pleasant Gregorian chant it created the perfect atmosphere.

Conques has become a relatively touristy place, with souvenir shops and postcard salesmen. The steep streets are narrow and without cars. In a side-street we stopped for a chat with a Canadian couple. They found it incredible that we were walking to «this place in Spain», as they put it. We told them about the pilgrim route and our experiences so far. They found it overwhelming to meet two proper pilgrims, and we had to pose to enable their 12 grandchildren to see photographs of us when the grandparents returned to Vancouver.

A bottle of wine was waiting for us at the *gîte*. Allan had also seen the snow on the peaks, and had accepted that we were right. Serena and Richard had also arrived, and we shared our wine prize with them as an aperitif before dinner.

Mark and I walked down the steep hillside to have dinner in the restaurant by the Roman bridge crossing the river. This was the last restaurant from Madame Jalbert's Gourmet article. French restaurants often offer set menus at a set price. They normally consist of five courses. The starter might be a soup, pâté or cold meat. Both main courses are warm; the first a light course and the second something more substantial, like roasted meat or fish. Cheese is served before dessert and coffees are put on the table. Bread, water and wine are included in the set price, and are replenished throughout the meal. The food in the restaurant by the bridge in Conques was varied, savoury and good value for money.

The nave of the Cathedral of Sainte Foy in Conques.

The streets in Conques are too narrow for cars.

THE ROAD FROM CONQUES
TO CAHORS

The sun was about to rise above the ridge when we left Conques the following morning. The *pâtisserie* had just opened, and we stopped for breakfast outside a chapel on a hill at the bottom end of town.

When we had crossed the Dourdou river the path continued steeply uphill. The GR65 showed no mercy, there was always a steep climb just after we had eaten.

Halfway up we really did need a stop to catch our breath. A tiny chapel is built here, maybe to give the pilgrims strength to carry on up the hill?

On our way up we met Serena and Richard, and walked with them for the next couple of days. We talked about anything and everything, the adversities of the pilgrim roads and of our freshly gained experiences. We

Sunrise over Conques.

wondered why our right boots always dried quicker than the left when walking. All four of us had experienced greater problems with the left foot than with the right. A good explanation was hard to find, but maybe it was due to the curving of the road, since we were always walking on the left side along tarred roads. We had also noted that our socks dried quicker when they were hung from the toe.

The weather along the French road was normally wet and chilly at this time in May. We had experienced a heat wave with temperatures close to 30°C, and after more than two weeks of blazing sunshine it was quite refreshing when a light drizzle set in.

Serena had heard me singing in the shower, and wanted to learn more about Norwegian culture. I told her the story of Mother Troll who had just put her eleven Troll children to bed, and sang the first part with gusto before I got the other three to join in on the «oja-oja-boffs» towards the end. Indeed I doubt if the song was giving them a greater cultural understanding…

In the town of Figeac we said goodbye to Serena and Richard. They were going to have a rest-day to exchange money and relax. Mark and I preferred places with fewer people, cars and noise, and continued towards Béduer instead. Maybe we would meet Serena and Richard again before reaching Santiago?

The *gîte* in Béduer was located on a campsite in the middle of the wilderness. After having inspected the grandeur of the place, we walked into the village itself to find a café. The village consists of a church, a general store, a café and nine houses lined along the road. The general store was of the good old style. A dim light bulb in the ceiling tried to light the dark interior, and it was almost impossible to tell what colour the walls were originally painted. The shelves were warped, and the old lady behind the counter had great difficulty reaching the tins on the top shelf. The selection of goods in local shops like this is limited, consisting mainly of fruit and vegetables stacked in boxes, canned food, dried food and simple toiletries, but they often have a friendly atmosphere that is not found in modern supermarkets. We got to buy what we needed, and sat down on the lawn outside the church to have our lunch.

In the evening we walked back to the village to have supper in the café. As the only guests we got the best table, and had a great view out over the valley and of the clouds hastily chasing above the landscape. While we devoured tomato soup with noodles, liver pâté and chops with spaghetti we discussed the journey so far. After two weeks each of us knew what the other was doing all the time. It was working extremely well, even if we both probably did certain things that irritated the other. Several of our mutual friends had predicted that we would not be on speaking terms after having been together constantly for more than two months. It was our task to prove these predictions wrong.

Back in the *gîte* we had been joined by five Frenchmen. They were about to cook supper in the kitchen next door to the dormitory, and garlic and wine seemed to be important ingredients in whatever they were cooking. We were off to bed, but they kept at it until late at night.

When they eventually went to bed they all immediately fell into a heavy sleep. Then the hullabaloo began. I have never heard anyone snoring as loudly and noisily as the four Frenchmen in our room! At least one of them needed to see a doctor about it. The fifth member of the group must have been aware of his snoring problem; he was sleeping in a tent outside the entrance, but we could hear him snoring through the wall, and it was almost drowning the noise from the other four. The penetrating noise was making it impossible to sleep, and we had not had much rest when our alarm clocks rang at half past five. Although there was just the remotest chance of waking up our room mates, we sneaked out of the dormitory to get ready for departure.

The temperature had crept below freezing, so we had a cold start to the day. Mittens were put on, but as shorts still made up the lower part of our walking outfit it was a cold pleasure walking through fields of stiffly frozen straw. The thick morning mist was covering the entire valley, and on the other side of the valley we could see a church tower sticking up from the sea of mist. Fortunately, the temperature rose considerably when the sun broke through.

The scenery changed again along the day's stretch, and became luxuriant and green with wood-clad hills and junipers. We had reach the limestone hills of Cajarc, and followed a steep country road down to the tiny town on the banks of the Lot.

The pilgrim roads were considered to be the roads to heaven, and we were beginning to understand why. The road seemed always to be ascending, and the descents seemed shorter and less steep. Nevertheless, we had come down from 1400 to 160 metres, but that may have had something to do with the curving of the surface of the Earth?

The town hall, *Mairie*, was closed, but we got our records stamped in the local art centre which was named after former president Pompidou. The *gîte* was on the first floor of an old building on the town square. Allan was a day ahead of us, and had left a message in the visitors' book about where to go for a cheap and tasty meal. We did not check the fridge, and missed the bottle of wine he had left behind for us.

Before bedtime Mark and I studied the tadpoles and newly developed frogs in the pond outside the old people's home. The French snorers arrived late in the evening, exhausted from the day's walking. All five were big and heavy, and did not appear to be in good physical shape. Luckily the *gîte* was divided into four-bedded rooms, and even if some of the loudest snoring could be heard through the concrete wall, it never got so noisy that we could not get to sleep.

In the village of Varaire we had planned to stay overnight in a *chambres d'hôtes*; Bed and Breakfast. After a day's march 24 kilometre long through rain we were looking forward to having a roof over our heads. Madame at the local bar explained that the *chambres d'hôtes* had closed down. The nearest overnight accommodation was in the convent in Vaylats, 10 kilometres further along the road. Mark and I in a convent, that sounded interesting! Madame called the monastery to reserve a room for two pilgrims, and we were soon on our way again. The intake of coffee had made us energetic, and we covered the 10 kilometres to Vaylats in good time.

From the outside the grey monastic building looked like an early 20th century prison. Tiny windows covered by pale blue shutters were the only details breaking up the monotone façade. Inside the walls there was a lawn, a garden and trees, so the building itself was giving a wrong impression of the place. We finally found the cor-rect entrance, and presented ourselves to two nuns. Sister Monique showed us to our quarters above the monastic bakery. She explained, smilingly, that *soeur*, Sister, is the best way of addressing a nun.

Our rooms had little in common with how we imagined a monastic cell to look. They were light and pleasant, and furnished with a desk, two spindle-back chairs and a wash basin. I must admit I was a little surprised to find large and soft double beds in a convent.

Supper was served in the Sunday School assembly room. Mother Superior wrote our names and addresses in her calendar before she solemnly stamped our pilgrim's records. She explained this was the first time they ever had a Norwegian pilgrim staying. English pilgrims were also infrequent visitors, and as a result we were treated as a rather exotic addition to the nuns' daily life.

Two elderly, lay ladies joined our company, and we entertained them in French to our best ability during the meal. Again we were served a varied and tasty five-course meal. Wine is a natural part of any meal in France, including those in the monasteries, and our two dinner partners insisted that we ate and drunk until the table was empty. That proved to be an impossible task, even for thirsty pilgrims.

The pilgrim route follows an old Roman road through a flat and characterless terrain towards the city of Cahors. The road was wide enough for us to walk side by side chat-ting, so we were making good time through the woods. We had very few provisions left, and what was left was consumed along the stretch to give us enough energy to keep going. There were no villages, shops or bars along that day's stretch, and although we passed the odd house every now and again, there were no people to be seen. Cows and dogs were also fairly scarce. The last 10 kilo-metres were a bit more undulating, and we had to walk down a steep descent to get to Lot and Cahors.

Lot is flowing in a narrow curve around Cahors, and the river had become considerably wider during its jour-ney towards the sea. We crossed it over the bridge Pont Louis Philippe, and walked down the wide boulevard which cuts Cahors in half.

Cahors is the capital of the regional *departement* of Lot. The city, with its 21,000 citizens, has given its name to the deep red Cahors wine produced in the region.

The Cathedral of Saint Etienne in Cahors.

The Tourist Information office helped us find moderately priced overnight accommodation. Hotel de la Paix; the Hotel of Peace, became our base for the next two nights. The hotel did not manage to live up to its peaceful name. The old building squeaked and groaned every time someone walked up the stairs or down the corridor. After the first night we renamed it Hotel de la Squeak.

We tried to have a rest-day every week to relax and catch up on some sleep. Even if the day was often spent meandering about looking at the local sights, our bodies deserved a rest from the rucksacks and heavy walking boots for a while. Also, there were always some practical tasks to accomplish, such as picking up depots, exchanging money and sending exposed rolls of film and used maps back home.

The rest-day in Cahors was spent looking over our equipment and provisions, supplementing articles we needed. We visited the cathedral of Saint Etienne, and while Mark was busy photographing the stained-glass windows, I took a closer look at the life of the market in the square outside. Afterwards we sat down on a corner to eat fresh strawberries and study French parallel parking

at its best. It felt as though we had been eating and drinking all day, so our energy reserves were undoubtedly replenished.

We spent the evening relaxing in a bar. Suddenly we discovered two familiar faces on the street outside: Serena and Richard! They had walked a long stretch of 40 kilometres that day, and were only one day behind us. Yesterday evening we had bumped into Allan again, he was still one day ahead. We tended to overlap each other on our rest-days, and kept in touch along the road by leaving messages at each overnight stop.

Saint James is in little evidence along this section of the French road. Apart from some small statues and stained-glass windows with scallop shell motifs, there is little to indicate that this was once an important pilgrim route. The background of the route was much more evident in the Massif Central. There even small bars were named after Saint James. Apart from our three English friends we had not met other Jacobean pilgrims, and we were often the only overnight guests in the *gîtes*.

THE ROAD FROM CAHORS TO SAINT-JEAN-PIED-DE-PORT

We were feeling energetic after the rest-day in Cahors, and crossed the Lot for the last time to continue towards the rivers Tarn and Garonne further south. The weather was changeable, and during the day we experienced one shower after another coming in from the West. We had reached the humid Atlantic climate. The wind was increasing in strength, the rain lashing against our bodies, and for the first time we had to put on our waterproof trousers. The luggage was well wrapped in watertight bags, and since we were appropriately dressed it was fairly pleasant walking in the rain.

As the day progressed the mud began to stick to the soles of our boots, making the walking quite heavy. We decided that perhaps it was time to find somewhere to spend the night.

We sought shelter from a heavy shower by a little chapel. Here we met two elderly French couples on a motor tour. While the rain was taking a short break, and Mark had taken a photograph for them in front of the chapel, we chatted about various subjects. We explained we had to start looking for overnight accommodation, and one of the Madammes knew of a monastery nearby which accommodated pilgrims. With our previous experiences of monastic life fresh in mind we decided to try to find this monastery, even if it was located a few kilometres away from the route.

A heavy rainstorm ensued, and although we were still fairly dry it was definitely time to get a roof over our heads. We reached the village of Escayrac, but saw no sign of a monastery, so we made a halt outside the village church to review the situation. While Mark emptied the

water from his boots, I went to find someone to ask for directions. A car stopped by the church to set down an old lady, and I walked over to the younger lady who was helping her out of the car. I put in use the standard phrase

Pilgrim in the chapel of Saint-Jean-le-Froid near Escayrac.

I had learnt for directions, and delivered it in a way that must have sounded perfect to any non-French speaking person. «Are you English», replied the younger lady in perfect English, my French phrase had obviously not been too impressive. Relieved that she spoke a language I was more familiar with, I did not give her a lengthy explanation about my national origin, and answered positively. She explained the road to the monastery, it was only around the corner.

We found the way easily, and pressed the bell outside the monastery door. The sign outside stated that this was a Dominican monastery dedicated to Notre-Dame. Our previous knowledge of the monastic orders indicated this to be a monastery for monks. You can imagine our surprise when the door was opened by a nun! We managed to explain our dilemma, and the Mother Superior came out to show us to the old school where we could stay. The amenities were very basic; a wash basin and a very basic pit privy in the hen-coop, but the place was bearable. We had plenty of room, and unpacked all our luggage to allow our rucksacks to dry.

Mother Superior, accompanied by a young Swiss nun, brought us supper. The young nun had spent two months walking from Switzerland to Santiago, and stayed a night at the convent on her way. In Santiago she decided to become a nun, and walked back here to begin her training.

The nuns invited us to take part in vespers, the evensong. Together with the seven white clad nuns we entered their simple, but atmospheric, chapel in the old stable. The whole service consisted of communal singing and readings from the Scripture. Mother Superior concluded with a prayer to the Virgin Mary, and asked that the two pilgrims would arrive safely in Santiago. It was a simple but graceful ceremony. No matter what belief one professes, the religious contacts are significant parts of the pilgrimage.

Next morning we took part in matins, the morning song, before getting ready to resume our journey. In a monastery you do not pay for board and lodging, but donate an appropriate amount. Mother Superior would not allow us to leave any gift for the convent. Smilingly she asked us to pray for the nuns in the cathedral in Santiago instead, which we naturally promised to do. Before we left she gave us a large tub of home-made honey for the road.

The sun had broken through again, but the track was still muddy from yesterday's rainfall. We were struggling up a steep hill towards a farm yard. Mark was walking in front along the slippery and narrow track. Suddenly a dog came chasing around a hedge, snapping at his thigh. It all happened so quickly that I did not understand what had happened until the Pointer-like dog had disappeared behind the barn.

«He bit me», said Mark. He had got two bleeding wounds in his thigh; one gash about four centimetres long and a deeper, rounder wound, probably from a canine tooth. The owner came running, and as the blood was already flowing from the wounds we took off our rucksacks to get out our first aid kits and dressing materials. Luckily, we had brought an extensive range of first aid materials.

Mark was cleansing and nursing the wounds, and put on a plaster with sutures to hold the gash tightly closed. In the meantime I wiped the blood from his leg, found the materials he needed and tried to assist to my best ability. The wounds were not looking good. They would have to be properly cleansed and stitched up by a doctor. Rabies is as good as eradicated in France, but it might be necessary to have a tetanus injection.

The dog's owner was distressed by the incident, but after we had managed to calm him down, he explained that the nearest doctor was in Lauzerte, five kilometres away. With Mark's thigh properly plastered and dressed we continued towards Lauzerte, supplied with a punnet of strawberries for damages in tort. Of course we should have asked the owner to drive us there, but we were so busy nursing the wounds that the thought did not occur to us until we had walked a fair stretch. Luckily, Mark was not having any difficulty walking, so we anticipated the muscles to be undamaged.

The medieval town of Lauzerte is located on a hill, and the GR65 follows a steep and crooked track uphill. Everything was closed for lunch in the town, including the local surgery. When it eventually opened we were immediately let in by the young female doctor. I followed into the office to talk to the patient while she was nursing the wounds. She plunged in a hypodermic containing anaesthetics, and prepared for the stitching. I had to find a way of distracting the patient, and started reading out words and phrases like «I have lost my wife» from my French

The morning light shows the road ahead from Lauzerte. ➤

Morning mist below Lauzerte.

The rivers Tarn and Garonne run as one towards the Atlantic Coast.

The pilgrim road across the market square in Auvillar.

large map of France stamped in post offices along the route, and when the journey was accomplished he would be writing a book about his adventure. He was walking at a good pace on his short legs. Every time we met we said goodbye, expecting to have seen the last of him, but for some odd reason we always caught up with him again.

Mark had to be a bit careful with alcohol due to the antibiotics. He was also running the risk of being photosensitive, i.e. sensitive towards sunshine and heat, and might get problems in the burning sun. We both agreed to take it a little easy for a few days to see how things developed. The following morning we were both feeling so restless that we ended up walking a stretch of over 33 kilometres. So much for taking it easy!

Below Lauzerte we passed a pond where croaking frogs, jabbering ducks and screeching crows were holding a deafening morning concerto. We found ourselves a more quiet spot in the woods to eat chocolate *croissants* and massage our toes. We examined our feet several times a day to prevent injuries and wear. Every morning we plastered them using sports tape, and lubricated them with moisturiser to keep the skin as soft as possible. Dead skin was cut off, and the nails kept short to prevent them from irritating the skin, making new blisters.

We had grown so accustomed to all the blisters we did not notice the small ones any more. They were generally left alone, and only dealt with if they began limiting our movements. I put a Compeed-plaster over the blisters to enable me to continue walking. These plaster-cushions held the blister in place and counteracted the pain, but they were so airtight that the blisters did not heal underneath. Some days the foot soles were like big blisters, and it felt like walking on broken glass. This was caused by a combination of the weight we were carrying, the velocity and the distances we were walking.

We continued for a few hours before taking a halt at the farm hotel Auberge Nouvelle. Whilst drinking our coffees the owner showed us a book in which other pilgrims had written their comments, and we had an amusing time reading about other people's experiences before adding our own. Blisters seemed to be a common problem for all pilgrims.

pocket dictionary. The pronunciation was not quite right, and the doctor seemed to be having minor problems keeping a straight face while concentrating on her task, but at least I managed to draw the patient's attention away from the needle and thread being pierced through his thigh.

Equipped with antibiotics, dressing materials and plaster we moved into the village *gîte*. The dormitory reminded me of an old hospital, but the entire *gîte* had recently been refurbished, and was comfortable. Our garments still damp from yesterday's rainfall were drying during the evening.

Not all the walkers we met were following in the pilgrims' footsteps. In the *gîte* in Lauzerte we became acquainted with Olivier, a stocky little Frenchman in his late thirties. He set out from Caen in Normandy on his Tour de France in April, and planned to walk through all the French *departements* before returning to Caen in October. He had his

The marking of the GR65 disappeared right after the farm hotel, and we did not find it again until we reached Moissac late in the afternoon. Instead we followed the route marked in our guidebook as closely as possible. Recently-built roads on the outskirts of Moissac made this difficult, but we managed to finally get there, found the Tourist Office by the abbey, got our stamps, met Olivier again and arrived at the *gîte,* totally exhausted!

The next morning we joined Olivier travelling uphill to Boudou to follow the ridge along the Garonne. The rivers Tarn and Garonne meet at Moissac to flow as one towards Bordeaux and the Bay of Biscay. We crossed a wide canal flowing parallel to the river, and followed the tarred country road through a flat, dull and featureless terrain. Walking along country roads was hard on our feet, and we were relieved when we could leave the road to follow a cart track instead.

On a farm we observed human life on the covered terrace outside the farmhouse. Politely we greeted Madame and Monsieur with *bonjour,* and they invited us over for something to drink, which we naturally accepted. As soon as we were seated they offered apple juice, grape juice and whisky. It was still before noon, so we decided to accept the grape juice. Whisky, this early and in this heat, may have given us an exciting boost to the day, but probably prevented us from reaching our destination.

We crossed the Garonne and continued southwards through a flat, repetitive and uninspiring countryside. In Bardigues we found ourselves in the middle of a *boule* tournament. *Boule* is an outdoor game similar to bowls, and the entire village was taking part in the tournament. We stopped outside the only bar in the tiny village, and over a couple of orange lemonades, Mark was still on antibiotics, we got talking to an English lady. She got married in the village church the day before, and was celebrating with the villagers during the whole weekend. We also met a young girl from Bermuda, but she seemed to prefer the tournament to chatting to two sweaty and not-so-pleasantly-smelling pilgrims. Olivier decided to stay behind to play *boule* while Mark and I walked the final stretch to the *gîte* in Saint-Antoine to spend the night there.

When undertaking a long walk it is often difficult to keep track of what day it is. Neither is it of any importance. Our

weeks seemed to consist of Wednesdays and Saturdays, the only days we managed to keep track of. With no itinerary to stick to, we approached the road one stage at a time. The tiny travelling calendar therefore remained unused.

In France most grocery shops, bars and restaurants are open on Sundays. On the other hand they are often closed on Mondays, which makes it a little difficult to buy something to eat.

We had run out of food the Monday morning we spent in the village of Saint-Antoine, but were hoping to find a *pâtisserie* in one of the first villages along the road. Our usual good fortune was not with us that day, everywhere was closed. While we shared our last bar of chocolate and drank a sip of water outside the church in Miradoux, we realised it might be our only meal along the day's stretch. While Mark was taking a quick reconnaissance round the village, I studied the map and guidebook to try to find a solution.

An old gentleman came walking by, noticed me and stopped for a chat. He switched into easily understandable English when his questions were becoming too advanced for my French. I explained that we were pilgrims on our way to Santiago, and were looking for something to eat. He walked on after a pleasant chat. Mark had not found anything interesting, and we prepared ourselves to walk on.

Then the old gentleman returned, and smilingly explained that he and Madame would be delighted to invite us for breakfast! We followed him down a side-street, and were soon seated at their kitchen table, where Madame was dishing up fresh bread, cheese, cooked meats and strong coffee. They also managed to get hold of a fresh *baguette* from a neighbour, and supplied us with whatever we needed for lunch. Their hospitality was overwhelming, and it almost became too much, so we explained that we were travelling on foot, and therefore could not carry too much with us. Any kind of payment was out of the question, our hosts saw it as their duty to support pilgrims. We tried to return their hospitality by showing them our pilgrim's records and tell them about our experiences along the road. «Again a pleasant visit to a French home», I wrote in my journal.

On French farms dogs, hens and cockerels are left to roam

freely. After the dog attack we kept a close eye on the dogs, and always carried a couple of pebbles in our pockets and had our walking sticks ready in case the dogs should get too close for comfort.

It is not necessary to hit the dogs to scare them off. Often it is enough to throw the pebbles towards them, or to stoop as if to pick up a stone. Through one farmyard we were followed by two hot-tempered Spaniel-type dogs. Their continuous barking got on Mark's nerves, so he eventually scared them off. We had become more careful, but luckily the four stitches in Mark's thigh were not causing him much trouble.

The village of Castelnau-sur-l'Auvignon was totally demolished on the 21st June 1944, in revenge for French resistance activities in the area. It has been completely rebuilt, and stands as a monument to the atrocities of war. Here six English ladies were having a combined strawberry and sightseeing break. They were spending a week walking

from Moissac to Nogaro, and were on more of a holiday than a strenuous walk. Some days they had sent their rucksacks ahead by taxi to walk their daily stretches of between 16 and 17 kilometres as lightly as possible, even if their packs only weighed 7 to 8 kilograms. When the ladies walked on we found a place in the shade of a tree outside the school to have lunch.

According to the map there was a short-cut across a tiny valley ahead, and we followed the country road marked with bleak versions of the red and white flashes. What the map did not show was that the valley had been dammed up, so the route disappeared down into the lake! Tired, and running on our reserve batteries, we had a quick, tempered discussion about where to go, before we unanimously decided to hurdle the electric fence and follow the cattle track along the lake back to the GR65. We undoubtedly needed a break. After four days of walking approximately 30 kilometres each day we noticed a certain lack of energy, and we were both looking forward to a rest-day in Condom.

Our little detour along the lake made us overtake the English ladies again, and we kept them company along the rest of the road to Condom. The ladies were going to stay in a hotel, so we left them to find our overnight stop.

Condom is a small city of 8,000 citizens. It lies only 75 metres above sea level, and is therefore one of the lowest points along the pilgrim road. The city is the centre for the production of the spirit Armagnac. The city's name has nothing whatsoever to do with contraceptives, even if the City Council is planning a contraceptive museum to attract foreign tourists.

The gîte was located on the top floor of an old school, with good facilities like a kitchen, showers and comfortable beds. Allan was waiting for us with cold beer in the kitchen. He had expected us to reach Condom that day, and it was as always pleasant seeing him again.

We spent our rest-day visiting the Gothic cathedral and looking around the city. We also used the opportunity to renew parts of our equipment. Mark needed new boots, and our socks were in need of replacing. We spent the af-

Stained-glass window from Nogaro.

The Holy Family, from Nogaro.

Saint Leon in the church in Navarrenx.

ternoon in the *gîte*, updating our journals and planning tomorrow's stretch. Mark was looking out of the window, and spotted Serena and Richard down on the pavement! We invited them up to have a look at the facilities.

They had noticed various medical wrappings and bits of dressing in the rubbish bins in a couple of *gîtes*, but were hoping they were not left there by us. We therefore had to tell them about the dog attack, the nuns and everything else we had experienced since we last met. In comparison, Serena thought that their pilgrimage was rather boring.

We all had supper together in an outdoor restaurant, and introduced the two new arrivals to *floc;* a dangerously tasty mixture of brandy and white wine. It was a pleasant evening with plenty of good food and lots of laughter.

The best way to learn a language is to travel and hear it in use. As we got used to the French pronunciation and managed to make ourselves understood by using simple words and phrases, it became easier to communicate with the people we met. The dictionaries were only used when we were really stuck. English was only spoken when others addressed us in English first. We had also learnt some of the basic phrases to ask for directions. "Left" is called *à gauche.* "Right" we never managed to remember, so we used *non-à gauche* instead. That worked well!

The great French-test occurred when we had to organise an overnight stay in a Roman villa. A farm nearby offered evening meals, but it was necessary to reserve a table in advance by phone. I prepared myself for what to say before dialling the number, but was a little startled when a child's voice answered the phone. Hopeful I asked for Madame, and when she was eventually put on the line I first explained that I did not speak much French before I reserved a table for two for eight o'clock, *non problem!*

The house where the archaeologists were staying during the excavations of the Roman villa had been made into a *gîte*. The villa itself was just on our doorstep, and the entire outdoor complex, with mosaic floors and baths, was open to the public. We almost felt like exhibits our-

Ancient waymark.

selves, since the tourists had full view into the *gîte* on their tour around the villa.

The meal at the farm was outstanding, the best since Madame Jalbert. Madame laid a large oak table in the dining room, and served us noodle soup, various pâtés and roasted pork with courgettes and mushrooms. For dessert we were served chocolate cake with custard. All ingredients had been organically produced on the farm. The wine was made from grapes she was growing behind the farmhouse, and a large pig was apparently happily rummaging amongst some vegetables in an enclosure behind the barn. We were in the company of three French cyclists from the Alpine region, and chatted with them while helping ourselves to the delights on the table. When everything had been devoured it was time for bed. We stumbled past the pigsty, along a field and across a meadow before it became too dark.

The night was peaceful. We were only disturbed by a black cat slipping in through the open window. I had obviously occupied her bed.

The pilgrim route was steadily taking us southwards, and we passed tobacco fields and the odd banana plant along the way. The first bullfighting arena was seen in the village of Manciet, and various signs indicated we were about to enter a region different from the previous ones, we were about to enter the Basque country.

When we arrived at the *gîte* in Nogaro, Madame in reception was almost more interested in telling me about her visit to her cousin in Evje, Norway, than in showing us the facilities. She was more talkative than my knowledge of French could cope with. Allan and Olivier were also present in the *gîte*. We had covered two days' walking in one, and they were obviously surprised to see us again so soon. Olivier was having problems with his stomach, and had taken it easy for a couple of days.

Over the next few days we walked through the towns of Aire-sur-l'Adour, Arsacq-Arraziguet, Arthez-de-Bearn and Navarrenx. Some of the names were so French that we avoided pronouncing them for fear of offending the local population. May was almost over, the sun was shining from a cloudless sky, and the heat had become so intense that our boots were leaving prints in the melting asphalt paving. One day we hung our washing to dry over some grape vines when stopping for lunch. It was dripping wet in the morning, but dried now in just half an hour. The terrain was again flat and without character, so we increased our daily stretches to reach our next great aim; the Pyrenees.

After four weeks along the road we had tried almost all the Camemberts we had seen on sale. We had also tried most types of salami and pepperoni sausages available. We had grown so used to walking that the long daily stretches were covered without difficulty. Our physical strength had improved considerably, and after a rest-day the body was longing to get going again. The first fifteen minutes in the morning were the worst, then the stiffness eased. Blisters were a part of our daily life. They caused us to limp, which in turn was leading to an unequal walking movement, which was causing fatigue. When we changed into sandals in the afternoons and strolled around without rucksacks, the limping was at its worst.

The walking was never boring. When the path was wide enough we walked side by side chatting, discussing or telling each other stories. Even on narrow tracks we kept the conversation going. However, there were days when we were in our own little world, with a need to reflect and wonder.

Various small tasks had to be accomplished along the way, like when we were wondering how long a stride we each took. From a road sign showing 150 metres to the next crossroads we counted how many strides it would take to the stopping line by the crossroads. To cover 150 metres we took 145 strides, which made each stride just over a metre long. We were therefore taking 97 steps over a 100 metre distance, and during our 1,500 kilometre long walk from Le Puy to Santiago we would be taking approximately 1,455,000 strides. Both knees were bent for every stride, so we would be bending them 2,910,000 times before we arrived. No wonder our feet were sore and our boots a little worn!

Early one morning, whilst walking over a hilltop, we got our first sight of the Pyrenees! It was a great feeling. The pointed peaks were capped with snow, and although the mountains were still some distance away, the sight spurred us onwards. The Pyrenees were our first major goal. When we got there we would be halfway, and

Animal life in the Pyrenees.

could start on the Spanish pilgrim route; the Camino de Santiago. During the day we passed the first road sign pointing towards Santiago. «Santiago 924 km» it said, we were getting there!

Road signs in the French part of the Basque country are in two languages; French and Euskara; Basque. The Basques are proud of their culture in a way that we Norwegians can only dream of. The farms are well maintained, and bulging window boxes are often placed outside the white and burgundy painted houses. The black Basque beret and the ball game of *pelota* are typical of the region. The purpose of the game is to strike a hard leather ball against a high concrete wall using a racket. Slogans like «Viva ETA» are often painted onto walls and sheds, but the Basque separatist movement receives little support here north of the Pyrenees.

The weather was grey and chilly when we reached the Basque country on the last day of May. Scattered showers

caused us to leave our raincoats on top of our rucksacks, but after a while it was raining so heavily we had to put them on. When the downpour became more like a flood we decided it was time for lunch, and sought refuge in a bus shelter. During a short interval between the showers we continued to the nearest petrol station, where we ended up having coffee in Madame's dining room. Like the true pilgrims we were, we took the shortest route to Saint-Palais.

The town of Saint-Palais is situated a little off the historical pilgrim route, but we made a detour there because the local Franciscan monastery was providing shelter for pilgrims. The monastic building is built in a square, with cloisters surrounding the monastic garden in the middle. There are now only three monks resident here, and the eldest was the only one still wearing the traditional brown cowl. The monks had employed a housekeeper to take care of secular matters like cooking and cleaning.

Franciscans do not have a hierarchy-based organisa-

tion in their monasteries. Everyone is addressed as *ami;* friend, whether monk or pilgrim. When signing our names in the guest-book we noticed the monastery had not had many visitors so far this year. We were the only pilgrims, and had the large *dormitorium* to ourselves during our stay.

The monks invited us down for supper in the *refectorium;* dining hall, and served us Basque rustic fare in large quantities. During the meal we talked about monastic life, the Basque country and the Basques' distinctive language and culture. The youngest monk offered to teach us Euskara. He said it was an easy language to learn, it would only take us a month. We unfortunately had to leave it for another occasion.

Next morning we had our breakfast at Stéle de Gibraltar, a boundary stone erected to mark the spot where the pilgrim routes from Paris, Le Puy and Vézelay come together. The Pyrenees had disappeared into the low cloud, but what we could see of the countryside along the route reminded me of south-western Norway, with rolling hills in lush shades of green.

Saint-Jean-Pied-de-Port was our last stop on the French side of the Pyrenees. The name means Saint John at the foot of the pass, and the town is located by the foot of the most difficult of the two pilgrim routes over the mountains. When a larger group of pilgrims was approaching the gate of Porte Saint Jacques, the townspeople used to ring the church bells to welcome them. Our arrival was quite unobserved by comparison.

The old part of town is picturesque, with small houses and long, narrow streets. The river Nive flows outside the old town walls, and those who take a look can see the trout swimming lazily beneath the Roman bridge.

Saint-Jean is also the assembly point for pilgrims starting out from the Pyrenees. Madame Debril is the local representative of the French pilgrim organisation. She is an authoritative old lady, and one of the great personalities along the route. Besides her stamping and approving our pilgrim's records she is a mine of information. Her office is full of books and leaflets about the pilgrim roads and the

cult of Saint James. The scallop shell motif is found on all the bric-a-brac filling the rest of the room. Ashtrays, letter openers, book supports, mugs, vases and other ornaments are all decorated with shell motifs. She was wearing a large shell pendant around her neck, and we somehow thought her use of the symbol had gone slightly too far.

Madame Debril is reputed to be a little strict and difficult. She is said to be particularly strict on only allowing one night in her tiny hostel. We were offered two, so we must have made a good impression. Maybe she considered us to be veterans after having walked half the total distance?

We used the opportunity to have a rest-day in Saint-Jean. Allan was also in town, and we would be seeing him every day for the rest of the walk. On one of our many strolls about town we bumped into Olivier again. He would be continuing along the route GR10 towards the Mediterranean, and so for the final time we said our fond farewells.

My walking boots were close to striking their last chord, and since the local sports dealer had a wide selection of large sizes, I would be wearing new boots over the mountains the following day. A dry-cleaner was given the challenge to get our shorts as clean as possible, while the rest of our clothes were hung outdoors in good drying conditions. I had a lively chat with the lady next door while hanging my laundry on a washing line. I did not understand a word she said, but agreed to everything until I realised that I was placing my laundry on her line!

The third depot-parcel was sent to the post office in Saint-Jean. Little did we know that it had been stopped by French Customs and returned to Norway. All information about the Spanish route was in that parcel! We tried to have it sent back down again, but realised it would be too long to wait. It was not a catastrophe, we had got maps and other accessories for crossing the Pyrenees, but it would have made the rest of the journey a little easier. Now we would have to rely on finding any necessary literature south of the mountains, and took notes from other people's books to have some information about the road ahead.

On the last evening we moved from Madame Debril's tiny hostel to the somewhat larger pilgrim refuge, to be ready for an early start the next morning. A group of eight

German students were also going to cross the mountains, and we became acquainted with Curtis from the USA. Curtis had initially tried to follow the route from Tours, but after two weeks he had encountered so many difficulties that he had caught a train to Saint-Jean instead. His walk had a deeply religious foundation, and he seemed to be lacking any practical travel-experience. His sister packed his rucksack for him, and from its contents one would not expect there to be any shops in Europe. He was also in bad physical shape, with too many kilos to carry. Now he was very worried about the following day's crossing of the Pyrenees.

Curtis had obviously been missing English-speaking company, and was beginning to rely on Mark and me. We tried to be pleasant and helpful without being patronising, and gave him advise about what he might be needing for the rest of his journey. Regardless of who you are or what background you come from, everyone is a member of the community along the pilgrim roads, and it is important to help and support each other along the way.

THE ROAD OVER THE PYRENEES

Dawn was breaking over the mountains to the east when we left Saint-Jean to cross the Pyrenees. Saint-Jean lies about 180 metres above sea level, and the 26 kilometre long route over the mountains reaches 1480 metres before steeply descending into Roncesvalles on the Spanish side of the border. This pre-Roman route is called Route Napoléon, and is the route followed by Charlemagne when he withdrew from Spain in year 778. At the summit the Emperor planted a cross and knelt in the direction of Santiago. The medieval pilgrims used to leave crosses made of palm branches to commemorate this event, and to ask the Apostle for a safe journey.

The weather was grey with a light drizzle, but the rain eased as we climbed uphill. The road runs wide along

Sunrise over Saint-Jean-Pied-de-Port.

steep, fern-clad hillsides for the first few kilometres. It is well waymarked with the usual red and white GR-marking.

We crossed a brook, and the wide road became a narrow path. Even though I was keeping a constant eye on the map, it must have been a moment's inattention at a path divide which had caused us to be balancing along a narrow track on a very steep hillside. We finally realised this could not possibly be the marked route, even a sheep would have problems balancing here. The Pyrenees are not the wisest place to get lost, but where were we?

A large old tree was well secured to the downgrading slope, and with our feet well supported against the tree we got enough balance to study the map. By comparing it to the terrain we found out where we were. The path followed the ridge a few hundred metres further up, so we managed to get back on the right track again.

A shepherd was guiding his goat-herd across the grassy hills, and a few sheep were grazing by the road. Further up we encountered a herd of horses. They were obviously used to walkers, and stood calmly looking at us as we passed them by. The Pyreneean vultures were nowhere to be seen. We passed a couple of barns and a mountain farm smelling strongly of goats, other buildings do not exist here.

Higher up the clouds had descended so low that we were walking in a veil of mist. It was not a thick mist, but enough to reduce our view to a couple of hundred metres. What we saw of the Pyrenees was not impressive for someone who grew up in Norway. The mountains are round and green, and the pointed, majestic peaks we had glimpsed earlier were conspicuous by their absence.

We suddenly came upon a Swiss couple we had first met in Saint-Jean, where we had an interesting conversation with them in a gibberish mixture of English, French and German over a few beers in a pavement café. They were both somewhere in their fifties. He was tall and skinny with long, greyish hair and beard, while she was plumpish with her face hidden behind dark sunglasses. Every time they took a break they had a smoke, and so a considerable number of breaks were taken during the day. They

View from the Pyrenees.

had their two dogs with them, and would be bringing them all along the road to Santiago. He was carrying all the luggage, including the dogs' food, in a tiny rucksack. She was responsible for the dogs and herself. Monsieur explained on a later occasion that Madame was seriously ill. We understood her to be suffering from a fatal disease, and that the pilgrimage to Santiago was something she wanted to accomplish before she died. Whether they ever made it to Santiago or not we never found out.

The actual border between France and Spain is marked by four rows of barbed wire. We crossed it via a cattle-grid at border post number 199, and congratulated ourselves on having completed the first half of the walk. There were no official insignia telling us we had reached Spain. Although we were not expecting a large border crossing with passport control and duty-free goods, we would have appreciated a sign welcoming us to Spain.

Port de Cize was the high-point of the day's stretch, 1480 metres above sea level. From here the road descends steeply towards the lowlands at 900 metres. The cloud had broken slightly, and we had wonderful views over the region of Navarre and the monastery at Roncesvalles in the valley below us.

My new boots were just fine until we started on the descent. My big toes began rubbing against the tip of the boots, and it became a slow and painful descent. Were the boots too small? I almost did not dare to think about it, and regretted having thrown my old ones away.

The monastery of Roncesvalles was founded as a pilgrim hostel in the 12th century, and developed into one of the most powerful monasteries along the road to Santiago. The need for a safe place in the mountains was considerably stronger in the Middle Ages, when roads and equipment were much simpler than today. In those days the monastery provided both a barber and a cobbler to take care of some of the pilgrims' needs. The monks here are still offering travellers board and lodging. Walkers with a

The monastery in Roncesvalles.

Cloisters in Roncesvalles.

valid pilgrim's record are able to stay overnight in the monastic dormitory. Other travellers can choose between the youth hostel or one of the two monastic hotels. The place is rather touristy, and the price level likewise.

We arrived in Roncesvalles in the afternoon, and registered with the vice-abbot before moving into our first refugio, one in a network of pilgrim hostels built in Spain over the centuries. The standard varies considerable, and you do not pay a set price per night, you donate a suitable amount. Today it is usually 200 pesetas, approximately 1 pound, per night.

The monastery church is dedicated to the Virgin Mary, and every evening a pilgrims' mass is celebrated here. The mass was concluded after all pilgrims present were summoned to the altar to receive a special blessing, and the priest prayed for our safe arrival in Santiago. This blessing dates back to the 10th century, and is regarded as one of the religious highlights along the road.

In the monastic souvenir shop we bought a map book to take the place of the one that never made it to Saint-Jean. Now at least we knew where to walk for the next couple of days.

Curtis had had a strenuous day, and was exhausted after the German students had kept him in front of them across the mountains. I had my doubts as to whether he would make it all the way to Santiago. If he did it would be a major achievement for him, and he would have learned a lot about himself along the road. I was hoping he would succeed.

During the evening more pilgrims arrived, both walkers and cyclists. Spaniards made up the majority, but several nations, and most age groups, were represented. In France we were often the only overnight visitors, now we had to get used to being surrounded by more people. We were halfway to our goal, and slept well in a packed refugio this first night in Spain.

≺ The cloisters in Roncesvalles.

Sancho the Great leading Christian troops in battle against the Moors. From the monastery church in Roncesvalles.

THE ROAD FROM RONCESVALLES TO BURGOS

We left Roncesvalles early in the morning to avoid the horde of other pilgrims. After five weeks we had got approximately 750 kilometres left to walk. With an average distance of 25 kilometres per day it would take us 30 days before we would arrive at the grave of the Apostle. My new boots felt hard against my soles, and I did not quite manage to keep the same pace as before. I gritted my teeth, and looked forward to a pair of new insoles to solve the problem when we got to the next city.

The scenery does not change immediately south of the Pyrenees. The road winds through woods and along fields, and the terrain looks more like the lower valleys in Southern Norway than the impressions most of us have of Spain. In the lowlands the differences from France are more noticeable. The climate is drier, and the buildings have more of a Spanish feel to them.

Several things were different along the Spanish part of the route. In France, we could walk until late in the afternoon, only stopping for a long lunch break to avoid the midday heat. In Spain, the June heat and the siesta forced us to change our daily routine. We still started walking at sunrise, but as the temperatures crept past 26°C around midday, we either had to try to reach our destination before lunch, or had a long siesta until the temperature was tolerable again. Between two and six in the afternoon the heat was practically unbearable. Although we always carried enough water and drank what we needed, our energy level was being considerably reduced by the heat.

The waymarking gradually changed. The red and white flashes from the GR65 continued through Navarre to Rioja, but painted yellow arrows were gradually taking over. The Spanish pilgrim organisation Los Amigos del Camino de Santiago are responsible for the marking. The yellow arrows are easily spotted, but the distance between them varies from region to region. The Spanish authorities spent a considerable amount upgrading the route prior to the Holy Year of 1993, and new signs with the scallop shell motif in blue and yellow were erected along the route. These signs are intended for walkers, cyclists and motorists, and are in addition to the other waymarks.

The greatest difference was having to get used to the Spanish language. It was confusing at first, but improved as we heard it in use and learnt the basic words. The short evening course I managed to attend before we set out had given me a useful foundation. Many Spanish words are similar to the equivalent in Norwegian or English, and when reading them we could manage to decipher what was being described.

The old Basque capital of Pamplona was the first larger Spanish city we reached. The city, with its 200,000 citizens, is the capital of the autonomous region of Navarre. It is probably best known for the fiesta San Fermin in July, where men can demonstrate their courage by running in front of the bulls that are let loose in the narrow streets in the old part of town. A large number of foreigners travel to Pamplona to take part in the fiesta, and the locals are always expecting some German or American visitor to be killed during the running of the bulls. Pamplona is also the birthplace of Ignatio Loyola, the founder of the Jesuit Order and the Spanish Inquisition.

We had a great view over the old parts of town and of the cathedral on our way into the city centre, and we walked past the bullfighting arena to take a closer look at the Gothic cathedral. Its interior is light and well kept, but the façade is classical, grubby and unattractive. We got

The Cathedral of Pamplona.

our records stamped before using the opportunity of being in a larger city to purchase a pocket dictionary and new insoles amongst other necessities.

The yellow arrows led us through the city by way of the university campus, over the motorway and to the *refugio* in Cizur Menor. Señora Roncal runs the hostel here as her hobby, and we enjoyed a superb hospitality, a large garden and comfortable beds in the annexe by her house. Allan joined us for supper. Later in the evening we were joined by Curtis, who entertained us by recounting his torments since the last time we met. We encouraged him to continue walking.

The last week before crossing the Pyrenees some of the excitement of dining out had disappeared, as we had begun to understand the descriptions on the menus. Now we could indulge ourselves again, and ordered the courses with the most melodious names. For dessert we did the

same, and Mark's face displayed a big grin when the waitress placed a large piece of ice cream tart with whisky sauce on the table in front of him. The expression changed rapidly when she realised she had made a mistake, and exchanged the tart for a bowl of dried walnuts!

West of Pamplona the green hills are replaced by sun-bleached hillsides, and the vegetation shows that little rain falls in this part of the country. From the Alto de Perdón ridge we caught a last glimpse of Pamplona and the Pyrenees behind us before descending into the Puente la Reina valley.

We left the GR65 in Muruzábal to follow the last stretch of the pilgrim road from Arles past the church in Eunate. This is a beautiful, little octagonal church surrounded by low cloisters. Whilst waiting for the coach-load of German tourists to complete their mass, we sat in the shade eating lunch with Allan. The tourists started leaving the church, and, like curiosities, we pilgrims were filmed and photographed from all angles. A couple of

≺ *Landscape south of the Pyrenees.*

Interior from the Cathedral of Pamplona.

Pamplona disappears in the heated haze behind us.

The church of Nuestra Señora in Eunate.

The Queen's Bridge across the Arga river.

tourists were curious enough to start talking to us. They were wondering how we were all related. It was obvious that Mark and I were brothers, or at least cousins, but was Allan our grandfather? While they were eagerly discussing our apparent kinship, a lady with a video camera was filming close-ups of Allan and his rucksack. Her filming became rather intrusive, but she did not see any need to ask for permission. We were feeling just like animals in a zoo!

We walked along yellow wheatfields to Puente la Reina. This is where the Spanish road, the Camino de Santiago, begins. The four North-European pilgrim routes join slightly west of the town, and continue as one road, a *camino,* westwards to the grave of the Apostle.

Puente la Reina, the Queen's Bridge, was founded sometime in the 11th century, when the queen, Doña Major de Sanches of Navarre, financed the building of a pilgrim bridge across the Arga river. Today the town has 2,000 citizens, and even if the handing out of bread, wine and milk to pilgrims ended a few centuries ago, the town is well worth a visit. A couple of storks were collect-ing twigs for their nest on top of a tall chimney on a fac-tory by the bridge. They were probably having a full view of everything happening below their high viewpoint.

The morning routine was now so well established that we woke up before our alarms went off at twenty past five. The Camino crossed the Queen's Bridge to follow a cart track westwards. We stopped in Ciraqui to visit the church, and I let myself be overwhelmed by the rich-ness of detail in the Moor-inspired portal. We continued along an old cobbled Roman road past vineyards. The last four kilometres towards Estella were walked along the main road. It was late in the morning, and the heat provided a good excuse for a quick stop in the first bar we found before continuing on into the town centre. We met yet another group of German tourists, and they were deeply impressed at meeting pilgrims on foot this far from Santiago.

Mark needed to buy a thin fleece jacket, and while he was looking at the range in a sports dealer's, I was keep-ing an eye on the rucksacks on the pavement outside.

Saint James's Church in Puente la Reina.

A *The pilgrim road west towards Ciraqui.*

Details from the church of Santa Catalina in Ciraqui. ➢

Modern relief in the main street of Estella.

Children from the local primary school were on their way down the narrow main street, and since I do not look typically Spanish they called out «hello» to me. On answering, they asked where I was from, and were evidently impressed by my height of 196 centimetres. The whole street was turned into an uproar of children calling and shouting. People in the shops and along the street were stopping to find out what was going on, and I was feeling quite like our king on the Royal Palace balcony on Norwegian Constitution Day.

Aimery Picaud was a cleric from Poitou in France. He is believed to have been the author of the Codex Calixtinus, the world's first travel guide. It was written in the 12th century, and is the earliest description of the pilgrim roads to Santiago. The book splits the road from the Pyrenees into thirteen stages, and gives advice on overnight stops, food, wine, good drinking water and poisonous rivers along the route. Aimery Picaud is very critical of most places along the Camino, and the peculiarities of the local population are often described in unflattering language.

Estella is described as a good place for accommodation, good food and good wine. The next *refugio* is supposedly located far from anywhere to eat, so we decided to eat a proper lunch in Estella. Our choice was a restaurant on Plaza Mayor which proved to be of a nobler kind, with white tablecloths and silver candleholders. Señora was not looking very pleased at the prospect of having three sweaty and dusty pilgrims with large rucksacks as her guests. We were feeling slightly out of place, and restrained ourselves from carrying out our customary toe-inspection during lunch. The hostess was becoming more hospitable as the meal progressed, and looked a bit startled when the meal was paid for with a Gold Card from The Bank of Hong Kong.

After we had eaten we continued on to the monastery of Nuestra Señora la Real in Irache. Just outside this monastery lies one of the most popular halts along the pilgrim road; a wine fountain. The fountain is free for pilgrims to use. Two taps are mounted in the wall, one for water and one for red wine. A wineglass and a mug are in place, ready for us to drown our thirst. Red wine straight from the tap was a new experience for most of us, but to be completely honest; the water tasted best. The wine was slightly on the young and immature side, but it improved

The wine fountain in Irache.

The monastery of Nuestra Señora la Real de Irache.

after a few sips. A statue of Saint James keeps an eye on wine-drinking pilgrims from a niche in the wall, and a sign encouraged us to «drink a sip of wine and toast our health».

The wine fountain is of a much later date than the monastery of Irache, which was founded more than a thousand years ago. Veremundo, the patron saint of Jacobean pilgrims in Navarre, was once abbot here, so we felt obliged to stop and have a look around. The gigantic monastic complex was turned into a university in the 18th century, and is today regarded as a national monument. It is undergoing an extensive, and much needed, restoration programme at the moment, to return it to its former greatness.

In the *refugio* in Irache we were joined by the German students. Curtis was still walking, but had decided to stay behind in Estella to rest for a couple of days. In the evening we sat chatting in the sun on the roof terrace. Our German friends were going to spend two weeks walking from Saint-Jean to Burgos. Thereafter they had to return to Rothenburg to complete their studies, this was some kind of warm-up to their exams. They had also found the wine fountain, and while they were drinking tap-wine we were eating what was left of the divine honey from the nuns in Escayrac.

The flat road winds between golden wheatfields, and a cooling breeze was making the heat bearable. My feet were sore and felt as though they were on fire, but we were nevertheless walking at a good pace to Torres del Rio. Here we stopped for coffee in a bar before finding Señora Lopez, who let us into the octagonal village church. Its interior is beautiful. The tiny church room is an octagonal vault with arches and motifs obviously inspired by Moorish culture.

We combined our lunch break with a siesta in the shade of an almond tree. The almonds were not ripe yet, so we only picked a few to taste.

Like most walkers, the German students were having a few problems with their feet. When we met them again along the road to the medieval town of Viana, one of the boys had got such big problems with his blood-stained blisters that he was walking the final 8 kilometres in his stockings. It did not appear to be causing him particular problems to walk without shoes, maybe his feet were al-

ready so numb that he could not feel the stony surface, but he could certainly do with a new pair of socks.

Viana is situated on a hill, and the road twists its way uphill towards the walls surrounding the old part of town. The *refugio* is next to the remains of a monastery, and has been completely renovated. Whilst hanging our laundry out to dry on a line in a small park I was accompanied by a group of young boys. After I had heard them counting to ten in English, they promised to keep an eye on the clothes while we were having supper. Viana was our last stop in Navarre, the following day we would be crossing the border to Rioja.

Logroño was the first city we walked through in Rioja. It lies by the river Ebro, and is a sizeable city with 120,000 citizens. South of Logroño is Clavijo, where the Christian troops fought against the Moors in 844. It was during this battle that James came riding out of the sky to decapitate 50,000 Moors. A statue on the façade of the church of Santiago el Real in Logroño shows James mounted on a charger as the great Moor-slayer.

So far we had not had any great success in finding an open post office to send home our last winter clothes, so we were planning to arrive in Logroño just before the post office opened. A toothless old lady stopped us along the road to get us to sign her pilgrim book. She explained that *Dia del Rioja,* the Day of Rioja, was celebrated that day, and therefore all shops and offices, including the post office, were closed. We walked through the city, and continued along vineyards westwards to Navarette and Nájera instead.

In the sandy surface along the road we looked for footprints. We could often recognise other pilgrims' footprints, and knew then who was walking ahead of us. Our new boots made it difficult for those following behind to recognise our prints, and later we were told it had caused some concern that we had just «disappeared» from the road.

In the Middle Ages a pilgrimage was used by several North-European countries as an alternative to a prison sentence. Belgian and German authorities are still using this alternative to remove juvenile delinquents and adolescents with behavioural problems from a hard-line environment. The walk gives them an opportunity to experience something positive, while at the same time being physically

Santiago Matamoros on Saint James's Church in Logroño.

challenging, which gives them an opportunity to see their life from a different perspective. A publicly paid guardian walks with them, and takes care of practical needs along the way.

Marika was a 16 years old German girl on her way to Santiago. She was taking part in an improvement project for juveniles with social problems. This was her final opportunity to improve on her life, the German social system would not offer her another chance. Now she had managed to lose her guardian, and had travelled for several days without money or papers. Naturally she was rather lonely and upset. She could not risk contacting the German authorities, in fear that it would end her journey.

We met Marika outside a supermarket in Nájera, and escorted her to the *refugio* where she could wait to see if her guardian arrived. Our winter clothes were finally sent off, and after our daily routine of washing our clothes, tak-

ing a shower and looking over our packs, we made the acquaintance of a young Spanish pilgrim. Lala is tall and dark, and had taken leave from her job in American Vogue to walk from Roncesvalles to Santiago. She was walking on her own, and was trying to follow the route her father walked in 1952.

Many familiar faces were turning up at the *refugio* during the afternoon. The two smiling and laughing Spanish ladies, the two older Spanish gentlemen who were impressed by our Spanish, the young Spanish couple and El Quiote we were to meet regularly during the rest of the journey. El Quiote had brought his mule Filipa. She was tied outside while most of us walked to the nearest bar to chat and cool down.

Marika came over after a while, and we talked with her about what she ought to do. We decided to visit the local police station to see if the police could locate the guardian. Lala was leading the way, since she spoke Spanish and English. She translated into English for me, and I translated into German for Marika.

The two local policemen were very understanding and helpful. They contacted the police stations nearby, asking them to check in hostels and *fondas;* small hotels, for a German woman fitting the description of the guardian.

The search was not crowned immediately with success. The police also had a dilemma; Marika was under age, and therefore not allowed to walk without supervision. They did not think it would be a good idea to keep her in their custody. The problem was solved when Lala and I were appointed «parents», with responsibility for Marika until the next morning. We asked her along on our sightseeing tour of Nájera, and she was clearly relieved and grateful that we were trying to help.

The monastery church of Santa Maria la Real is built over a fantastic cave in the red cliff overhanging the town. The cave was discovered in 1044 by the young king Don Garcia Sanches III. He was out hunting, and had just released his gerfalcon to catch a partridge. The partridge disappeared into the cave with the falcon chasing after it, and the king entered the cave in search of the birds. In the depths of the cave he found a statue of the Virgin Mary, a church bell, a lamp and a vase of lilies. The two birds were sitting calmly at peace next to each other. The king interpreted this as a celestial promise, and commissioned the building of the church. The statue, the bell, the lamp

The cloisters of Santa Maria la Real in Nájera.

Cloisters in Nájera.

and the lilies are all depicted in the altarpiece in the church. In the pantheon is a row of sarcophagi containing the remains of the sovereigns of Navarre, Castile and León.

Back in the bar there was much laughter when a Spaniard I was talking to pulled out a tape measure to prove that I am more than two metres tall. Lala and Mark

The Royal Pantheon by the red cave in Nájera.

were also measured. The Spaniards were obviously not used to seeing three such tall pilgrims together. We did in fact receive the nickname of Los Peregrinos Altos; the Tall Pilgrims.

We invited Lala to join us for a restaurant supper, and left it to her to decide what to order. For a change we knew what we had ordered before the food was placed on the table. We chatted about everything from Norwegian cuisine to Spanish nudism. We drank a house wine, which was full-bodied and pleasant. Rioja is one of the largest wine-growing regions in Europe, and the vineyards are producing more wine than they are allowed to

Detail from the monastery in Nájera.

export, due to EU restrictions. The overflow has to be consumed within the region, and table and house wines are therefore often of high quality.

Outside the *refugio* the police were waiting for us, and we followed them to the station. While we were waiting the guardian was found in a *fonda* in Los Arcos, 40 kilometres further east. The police constables offered to drive Marika there in the morning. They understood her situation was a little special, and collected her in a civilian car. They would not be reporting the incident to the German police, in order for Marika to continue along the road that might lead her to a better life.

The monasteries in San Millán de la Cogolla are located a fair distance from the Camino itself, so we caught a taxi to get there the following day. We had now been walking for six weeks, and it felt a little strange to be whizzing along at 90 km/h. The driver was playing gypsy music on the car stereo, and the ride became quite atmospheric.

There are two monasteries in San Millán. Suso, the upper, is a simple Visigothic monastery. It was built in the 6th century over a cave in which Saint Millán lived as a hermit. The monastery used to be inhabited by Benedictines, and houses the saints' tomb. The empty sarcophagus in green alabaster is still set in the cave. Yuso, the lower monastery, is larger and of a much later date. Even though a section of the monastery has been changed into a luxurious hotel, eleven Augustinian monks were still remaining in the monastic section of the complex.

A monk showed us, together with a large group of Spanish tourists, around Yuso. As soon as Padre Alfons learnt that we were pilgrims we were taken aside to be shown the real treasures. His guided tour was a journey through the life of Saint Millán and the history of the two monasteries, and with Lala's translation into English the visit became a great experience.

The remains of Saint Millán are kept in a richly decorated ivory coffer in a separate room. The original coffer is only shown to pilgrims, the tourists are shown a copy in an adjacent room! The books are kept in special bookcases built into the walls of the library. The pages were made of vellum, and each book weighs over 100 kilograms. My respect for the written word was renewed when I saw the skill used by the monks to create these richly ornamented treasures.

From San Millán we walked back to the Camino. Lala, Mark and I walked together, and kept the conversation going along the way. Since all three of us are of a marriageable age, it was natural that we discussed relationships and marriage. I found the courage to ask Lala to explain to me the mysteries of bullfighting. Although she is a vegetarian, she did not have any difficulties in defending this important part of Spanish culture. Bullfighting symbolises man's fight against evil. The bull is an evil animal, and deserves to die when the fight is over, she said.

A cart track over golden fields led us on to Santo Domingo de la Calzada. The sound of guitars, clapping and singing revealed that a gypsy family was holding a party in a barn on the outskirts of the town.

Santo Domingo is named after Saint Dominic, the Benedictine monk who spent most of his life building roads, bridges and hostels for pilgrims. When he died a cathedral was built over his simple chapel. The town which grew up around the hostel and cathedral is renown for being one of the most hospitable places along the Camino. The original hostel has been taken over by the Spanish state and turned into a *parador*, a fashionable hotel. We pilgrims were not suffering any hardship in the

Saint Millán fighting the infidels.

The sacristy in Yuso.

slightly simpler, but modern hostel by the cathedral, and were quite content.

Displayed in the hostel there were statistics about last year's pilgrims. Spaniards and Germans made up the majority, but the route is also popular amongst the French, Belgians, the Dutch and the English. From the Scandinavian countries there were mainly Danes registered. Only two cyclists appeared next to the Norwegian flag. Norwegians are generally absent along the pilgrim road.

Saint Dominic is buried in the cathedral. Here we also found one of the strangest phenomenons along the route; a large coop where a hen and a cockerel are strolling about! The birds are kept here to commemorate the young French pilgrim Hugonell. He was on his way to Santiago with his parents, and stopped for the night in a tavern in Santo Domingo. The landlord's daughter took a fancy to Hugonell, but when he rejected her advances, she sought vengeance by placing a silver cup in his saddle-bag. Hugonell was accused of stealing, found guilty and

hanged. His parents continued towards Santiago. On the way they heard Saint Dominic's voice telling them of Hugonell's innocence and that he was alive. They returned to Santo Domingo, and arrived just as the magistrate was about to have his supper. He stated that Hugonell was just as dead as the cockerel on his plate. Then the cockerel stood up and crowed! The magistrate was so shocked that he ran to the gallows, where he found Hugonell alive. He was immediately released, and all was forgiven.

Henceforth, from about the 16th century, hens and cockerels have been kept in the cathedral. Their feathers were supposed to bring good luck, so the fowls had to be locked in to prevent them from being completely plucked. The pilgrims also used to feed them to ensure a safe journey to Santiago. Those who hear the cockerel crow will see the tomb of Saint James, according to the legend. We had heard of pilgrims who had been waiting for several hours before this miracle happened, but the cockerel was apparently having a good day today, he was crowing continuously. That was a good sign!

Along the road from Santo Domingo de la Calzada we met El Quiote and Filipa again. Ten years ago his back was damaged in an accident, and the doctors gave him two alternatives; walk or be paralysed. Since then he has been walking. He has walked from Barcelona to Rome, and he has walked to Santiago several times. The donkey Filipa was carrying all their luggage. She could carry up to 30 kilos and walk a maximum of 25 kilometres a day at a slow pace. We found out that Mark and I beat her where speed and weight were concerned. An umbrella and a goatskin-bag with sweet red wine were important parts of their travelling-equipment. He was happily sharing the wine with other pilgrims. It had to be drunk the Spanish way, with a long, thin jet hitting in the middle of the throat.

The religious aspect of the pilgrimages is better expressed in Spain. Here we noticed the pilgrims' special status, and what a privilege it was to be able to go on a pilgrimage towards the end of the 20th century. James is the patron saint of Spain, and the road to Santiago is an important part of Spanish culture. A Spaniard should go on a pilgrimage at least once in his life.

The local population along the Camino have a friendly attitude towards pilgrims. As God's Travellers, the pilgrims receive advice, help and support along the road. We often had to stop for a chat and explain who we were and where we had come from. The simple Spanish words and

phrases we had learnt enabled us to keep the conversation going.

We were most comfortable in the countryside, away from cities and built-up areas. The cities were too large and noisy, and the population less friendly and more difficult to communicate with than the country folk. A pilgrim is someone walking along the road, and a simple country church often gave us more than a richly ornamented cathedral.

When the Camino ran parallel to main roads we waved to all cars driving past. The motorists often returned the greeting by waving or flashing their headlights, and truck drivers often gave us a honk of their horn. This all made the otherwise so tedious road-walking more enjoyable.

We met two older ladies and an old gentleman on the road through the village of Villambistia. «A pilgrim needs a staff», said the man in Spanish, and ceremoniously handed me his shepherd's staff. He asked me to take it to the cathedral in Santiago, and to pray for him there, which I naturally promised to do. Thus a part of him joined our pilgrimage. It was important to move the staff from time to time while walking, so both sides of my body got the same strain. It became a habit after a while.

In the afternoon we reached the village of Villafranca Montes de Oca, and stopped at the first and only bar to cool down before moving into the *refugio*. The hostel was Spartanly equipped, and for the third day running it was only possible to take cold showers. «A pilgrim's needs are simple», I wrote in my journal, «we are ecstatically happy when there is hot water in the shower and paper in the toilets». The Camino is the very symbol of all things spiritual leading us to the objectives of life, nothing must take the pilgrim's attention away from the road.

The morning mist lay humid and cold over the terrain when we left Villafranca at dawn. The road took us through a hefty forest towards the height of the Oca-mountains at 1150 metres. The road over the mountains used to be one of the most dangerous stretches along the medieval pilgrim route. The woods were thickly infested with wolves and robbers, and the stretch was described as a place through witch to «hurry and pray». When the pilgrims reached the monastery of San Juan de Ortega on the western side of the mountains they were safe.

Much of the forest was lost in a fire a few years ago,

The scallop shell shows the way to Santiago.

The belfry in San Juan de Ortega.

and we had seen neither wolves nor robbers before we arrived at the monastery. Saint Juan built the monastery here as a shelter sometime in the 12th century, and the priest guiding us around explained that the hostel can sleep up to 200 pilgrims. He took us to the church to show us the crypt containing the remains of Saint Juan. Several of the columns in the nave are decorated with beautiful and well maintained carvings. A carved figure of the Virgin Mary is placed so that it is only reached by the sunbeams for seven minutes at the vernal and autumnal equinoxes.

A pilgrimage is a spiritual experience. Whilst walking we had time to think and contemplate, and see life in a somewhat different perspective. We also got inspiration from what we saw and experienced, and whilst processing the impressions several strange ideas were appearing. On our way across the steppes towards Burgos, I reached

the conclusion that God is a personification of the sun, representing light, hope and all things positive in our existence. Everything divine is created by man. The divinity is therefore in ourselves, we have to reveal the most positive aspects of our existence to be able to see the light and the hope.

A pilgrimage may also be a symbol of life itself. The journey started in Le Puy. It matured along the way in France, where the body changed and was trained for the onward journey. The change from the French to the Spanish road showed the transition from the physical to the spiritual. The body is familiar with the daily routine, and we have more energy to think. On reaching Santiago we would reach our goal, and if we continued our journey westwards to Cape Finisterre, The End of the World, to see the end of the European mainland, the journey could only continue across the ocean towards the sunset, the end of life.

THE ROAD FROM BURGOS TO LEÓN

The Camino follows the main road for the last 7 kilometres through industrial estates and monotone suburbs into the centre of Burgos. The road is heavily used by large lorries, so we caught a bus along this stretch.

Burgos is the capital of the region of Castile. It is a modern industrial city with 170,000 citizens. The *refugio* had been moved to a park west of the city centre, and when we finally found it we were met by three smiling Señoras, who happily shared the remains from their picnic with two hungry pilgrims. In the hostel we recognised a pile of rucksacks; the German students had also arrived in Burgos. They were going to catch the next overnight-train back to Germany. Before saying our farewells to go and explore the city we promised to visit them in Rothenburg someday.

The Gothic cathedral in Burgos is one of the largest and most decorated churches in Spain. Amongst all the stained-glass windows, the sculptures, the images of the saints and all the other treasures stands a statue of Jesus. The statue is placed in a chapel at the far end of the cathedral, and is said to be modelled from the very body of Christ. It is covered in human skin and human hair, and the beard is apparently in need of a shave every eighth day. The statue is far from being handsome, and reminded me more of a badly stuffed animal from an old museum than a statue for religious worship.

Our depot was the largest parcel on the *lista de correos*-counter, and it seemed to beckon me when I walked into the main post office. The film stock had been running short over the past few days, but now we had enough to last us through the rest of the journey.

At the Tourist Office we bumped into Lala and Allan

again. They had decided to stay in a hotel. After a quick consultation we agreed to follow their example, and found ourselves a comfortable double room in a small *hostal;* a simple hotel. We washed our laundry in the bath tub, and, after some acrobatic movements out of the first-floor window, placed them in a suitable location to dry.

I was feeling exhausted after a long day, and was looking forward to a comfortable night's sleep. The following day we were going to relax, and could sleep until we woke of our own accord. That was a part of the rest-days that I thoroughly enjoyed.

From Burgos there is a bus-service to the monastery of Santo Domingo de Silos. The Benedictine monks here have managed to revive the interest for Gregorian chants. A few years ago they surprised the music industry by releasing a CD that went straight to the top of the European charts. A visit to the monastery was almost a must when we were in the area, so we decided to combine our rest-day in Burgos with a visit to the village of Santo Domingo.

The bus ride took one and a half hours. Both the bus and the driver were past their prime. The bus smelt of diesel, the clutch was due for replacement, the changing of gears a nightmare, the light panel above the aisle half loose and there were quite a few screws missing from the interior. Next stop was probably some remote village in the South-American mountains, the bus could hardly remain legal on European roads for much longer.

The priest in San Juan de Ortega had warned us against leaving the Camino de Santiago. He said we would lose some of the valuable insight we had achieved along the road, and advised us to stay on the Camino, the

Burgos Cathedral.

James thrones on top of Burgos Cathedral.

The cloisters of Las Huelgas outside Burgos.

real road. After having safely arrived in Santo Domingo de Silos we understood what he meant. Several coaches were parked in the village outside the monastery, and a crowd of people, mainly middle-aged Spanish ladies, were on their way into the monastery church. We found ourselves seats towards the front of the nave, while the tourists filled up any extra space. The noise was deafening, and only a few took notice of the sign requiring silence in the church.

The church is Romanesque, with a simple interior and large, empty walls. The evensong, vespers, began when one of the black clad monks came forwards to light the candles in the choir. The rest of the twenty monks arrived from the sacristy to find their places in the far end of the choir. All the prayers were sung in Latin, discreetly accompanied by an organ. The song was like velvet, pleasant and relaxing, and was best enjoyed with closed eyes and my head hanging low. My body began relaxing, and I freed my mind to wander far and wide.

Halfway through the service the singing was drowned by the noise from the congregation; the coaches were ready for departure! The Spanish ladies gathered their carrier bags and started leaving the church. The noise was deafening and completely destroyed the emotional atmosphere. The incident clearly illustrated the contrast between the secular and the spiritual, and the tourists were displaying a great lack of respect for other people and their work. The singing is a part of the monks' daily routine, not a circus performance!

When the singing was completed and the coaches gone, the village was deserted. Our bus back to Burgos was not leaving until the following morning, so we spent the night in a *hostal* outside the monastery walls.

Early next morning we were back in the church again to take part in matins, the morning prayer. Now there were only eight people present in the nave. It was as if the song was filling the entire room and my inner being. The tranquillity had taken over my body, and being half awake I was letting my thoughts carry me away. I tried to think good thoughts about those I care for, and could feel myself being filled with good emotions. Maybe this is what a prayer is all about? It does not need to be addressed to a supernatural spirit, but can be a reminder about what I find important, a way of stopping in an otherwise busy life. Sore feet and long daily stretches were all forgotten, and the service became a great experience.

On the bus back to Burgos I was trying to gather my thoughts. I wondered how I could become a better person, a better person towards my surroundings. One day, not so far ahead, the journey would be over, and we would have to return to reality. Before I fell asleep I decided to leave the future alone, and enjoy the present instead.

We continued from Burgos on the 15th June. Ahead of us lay a 175 kilometre long stretch across the Meseta, the desolate highland plateau covering the central part of Spain. The flat plateau is surrounded by mountain ranges, and the route follows cart tracks through the dry landscape, 800 metres above the sea. Trees and houses are few and far between, and it is difficult to find a shady spot

Waymark near Castrojeriz.

View from the Mostelares plateau, 1400 metres above the sea.

The road towards Castrojeriz.

Crosses show the way across the Mesa Colina de Mostelares plateau.

if we were not moving at all. The terrain was fairly monotonous, and dry wheatfields and sun-bleached meadows were all that we could see.

A shepherd dog was herding a flock of sheep across the barren plains. The shepherd himself was following the flock's movements from a distance. He was dressed in dark shirt and trousers, boots and a hat, and his weatherbeaten appearance indicated he had been herding sheep for many years. Under the hat I noticed a symbol of our modern civilisation; a pair of headphones. A shepherd's life must get a little lonely at times.

The heat was intense, and we stopped to cool down in a bar on the outskirts of the small town of Castrojeriz. Here we met Santiago; a well-dressed Spanish gentleman in his fifties. Santiago was walking between 60 and 80 kilometres per day, in an attempt to accomplish the thirteen stages in Aimery Picaud's Codex Calixtinus in thirteen days. He believed it was important to avoid getting obsessed by the road, and that one could only follow the Camino once in a lifetime. Walking it more often was only done to show off. His words were a strong contrast to other pilgrims we had met, who were doing this for the eighth or eleventh time.

We stopped for the night in the village of Itero de la Vega, where the medieval pilgrims used to kneel before a statue of James housed in one of the churches. A small house had been converted into a simple *refugio,* and the owner kept his hens and turkeys in the backyard. Fortunately, they remained quiet during the night, but at half past four the cockerel could not restrain himself any longer. He crowed to his best ability, and was not going to give in. When I awoke I was fully convinced that man started eating poultry to avenge all those early mornings.

The Knights Templar were responsible for the protection of pilgrims throughout the most dangerous regions along the road to Santiago. They organised safe pilgrim routes through Western Europe, and sometimes included visits to places of religious importance to boost the pilgrims' spiritual strength.

In the 13th century they built a church and a convent in Villalcázar de Sirga. The village which developed around the church became an important stopping place for the pilgrim traffic. The church exterior is today in a state of decay, with long cracks in the stone walls, but

on a hot day, so we were not exactly looking forward to crossing the plateau.

The sun was shining from a cloudless sky when we set off. Although a light breeze was removing some of the heat, we were sweating considerably whilst walking. We still started walking at sunrise, and calculated the stretches so we reached our destination before the heat got too intense at around two o'clock.

It was important to maintain our liquid balance. The water bottles were filled with cold water from the tap every morning, and we drank from the water fountains we came across. Still we had to stop in bars and cafés along the road to top up on liquid. The villages were sparse, and the selection of food and other supplies minimal.

The ridged hills on the horizon were the only fixed points in the flat terrain, and although we were keeping a good pace they did not seem to get any closer. It was as the interior is beautiful, with tall Gothic arches in a golden sandstone.

In Villalcázar we met Pablo Payo, one of the great characters of the Camino. He is a tiny man well into his nineties, and used to run the village hostel, the bar and the restaurant. Now he has left most of the daily running of the business to younger members of his family, and only appears on special occasions. The restaurant was in an old 16th century storage house, with dark, rustic wooden tables and benches along the walls. Whilst enjoying a light meal of dried meat, Spanish black pudding and *claro* wine we were accompanied by Pablo. He had put on his pilgrim's hat and cloak, and presented each of us with a scallop shell in a silk cord to carry around the neck. He also invited us to join a wedding procession from the church as soon as the wedding ceremony was completed.

We planned to have a shower and wash our clothes in the meantime, but did not manage to get that far before the whole village was gathering outside the church to toast the happy couple. Together with a drummer and a flutist,

Pablo was leading the procession, followed by a six-tiered wedding cake. The cake was carried on a sedan, and protected against the sun by a parasol. The entire village population followed the cake around the church before they attended the wedding reception in the Knights Templar's old refectory.

Next morning we dutifully carried the scallop shells we got from Pablo when leaving Villalcázar. They were fairly impractical to wear when walking, so we stopped behind the first little hillock to take them off.

The high midday temperatures made us consider the possibility of crossing the Meseta towards León at night. The terrain is even and the road is heading straight to the west, and should not be too difficult to follow. Together with Lala and Allan, we decided to try walking at night when it was chilly and starlit, and to sleep during the day instead.

Five kilometres from Villalcázar lies the town of Carrión de los Condes. This was our last stop before the planned night-walks. According to the legend, the church of Santa

Pablo Payo leading the wedding procession in Villalcázar.

San Martín in Frómista is one of the oldest churches in Castile.

The church of Santa María la Blanca in Villalcázar.

Landscape from the Meseta.

Maria del Camino stands on the spot where the rulers of Christian Spain paid their annual protection-money of one hundred virgins to the Moorish lords. We wanted to spend the day here relaxing and preparing ourselves for a long night's walk across the highland over the next forty kilometres to Sahagún.

We were drinking coffee in an outdoor café, watching a group of young girls decorating the street outside the church with floral motifs. An old lady explained that the street was preparing for the afternoon's procession in honour of Corpus Christi; the Body of Christ, which the entire population of the town would be attending.

The procession started from the old town bridge, and was led by a young boy swinging a large censer from side to side. Three other boys followed behind him. The boy in the middle was carrying a large silver cross, and the two on the flanks were each carrying a silver candleholder. Behind them followed several groups of men with large mono-coloured flags.

A little further behind the flags followed a flower-covered carriage, with a small silver statue of Christ placed on a richly ornamented platform. The carriage was pulled by two men. Surrounding the carriage were about twenty girls, approximately 8 to 9 years old, dressed in bridesmaid-like dresses. They were carrying baskets full of flowers, which they sprinkled over the carriage at intervals. Behind the girls followed several boys of the same age, dressed in naval uniforms with stripes and gold braids on their blue jackets. The children were on their way to the church to receive their first communion, an important event in the Catholic church.

Two priests dressed in white followed the carriage, and alongside it walked the inhabitants singing psalms. The streets were rather narrow, and from balconies draped with Spanish flags people sprinkled flowers over the procession. When they arrived at the church, all participants went in to celebrate the communional mass.

The procession had struck a cord in me. I was feeling a strong togetherness with the local population, and was feeling alive but totally confused. Tears were running down my cheeks. It was like a dam was breaking inside me, some kind of emotional purification. What do I want to get from my life? What am I looking for? I have so many questions, and am finding so few answers. It struck me how much belief can mean in daily life. The Catholics

have a positive outlook on their existence. Man is placed in the centre, and religious conduct is a simple and natural part of their daily life.

Our guidebook describes the 38 kilometres from Carrión de los Condes to Sahagún as a long and dreary stretch. The road runs through a barren terrain similar to the Gobi desert, and the open plain is so desolate that the few trees here are highlighted as major sights on the map. Bars and shops are far apart, so all supplies have to be bought in advance.

We left Carrión around ten in the evening. There was still some daylight, but it did not take long before darkness fell. For the first hour we followed a sporadically lit country road, but when we continued along a stony cart track we had only got the stars to light our way. Luckily, we did not need to worry about motor traffic, but we had put on our dangling reflectors to be on the safe side. When we passed the village of Calzadilla de la Cueza and were walking along the main road again, we noticed the cars were slowing down when they saw our reflectors. We were not using our torches, but trusted the night-sight of the person in the lead. The lead was taken in turns, since it was hard on the eyes having to concentrate for hours in bad light. I hardly saw the track itself, since I was concentrating on following Allan's white socks in the darkness before me.

Closer to sunrise it was getting easier to find our bearings. The hills in the horizon did not seem to get any closer, and it felt like we were walking in syrup. It drained our spirit, so instead of looking at the horizon I fixed my eyes on the road a few metres ahead. Then at least I could see we were slowly progressing. Sometime during the night we completed the first half of the road from Roncesvalles to Santiago. We had covered over 1,100 kilometres, and had less than 400 to go. In a way I was looking forward to arriving at Santiago, but in another I could continue like this for a good while longer. The journey itself had become more important than the goal. Maybe I did not really want to get there?

Night walks were hard on the legs, since we could not see where we placed our feet. In daylight we could vary our stride and follow the contours of the terrain. In the dark we stumbled allot, which strained the muscles. All four of us were exceedingly tired when we finally arrived in

The Corpus Christi procession in Carrión de los Condes.

Sahagún at around six-thirty in the morning. Exhausted and tired we moved into a *hostal,* and slept until sometime in the afternoon. The church bells were the only disturbance. They rang every quarter of an hour, and sounded like someone hitting a zinc bucket with a hammer.

Unfortunately, the road ahead to Mansilla de las Mulas did not promise to be any better than the road to Sahagún. Abbè Georges Bernès describes the next forty kilometres in this way: «Pilgrim, prepare to suffer: If you are to gain merit from your pilgrimage, this is the place for it».

Lala decided to stay behind in Sahagún to rest. She wanted to continue in daylight the following day instead; the first night became a little too eerie for her. The Spaniards believe the night has ears. Therefore we should talk as little as possible, and keep our thoughts to ourselves, whilst out on the open plains.

It was getting dark when the three of us left Sahagún. The moon and the stars were not up yet, but the path was covered in a layer of light sand and easy to follow. Tonight's stretch to Mansilla was 35 kilometres long, but less strenuous than the previous one. The route followed a gravelled track with young poplars planted along the left side. They will provide necessary shade from the sun when fully grown. The Charlemagne legend claims that the Emperor's army camped here on the banks of the river Cea before one of the great battles against the Saracens. The Emperor's knights set their lances into the ground before turning in. Overnight some of the lances took root and put out leaves. These were the lances of those who were to die in the forthcoming battle, a sign that they were to die as martyrs. The trees in the poplar woods outside Sahagún are supposed to originate from the lances which took root.

Along the road benches are placed at regular intervals, but fountains and other water supplies were nowhere to be seen. Lack of subsoil water is a probable reason why the Meseta is so dry. Any drilling has to go deep down, which makes the drops expensive. We were prepared for the lack of water, and filled our water bottles before we set off. The few villages we passed had water fountains, so with a little planning it was not a problem.

Several trains were trundling through the night along a railroad track to the north. The coaches were lit up inside, and looked like ghost trains when passing at a few kilometres' distance. The gravelled track became replaced by a wider tarred road. We had not met any traffic, and when it was time for a break we just sat down on our rucksacks in the middle of the road to enjoy sweet cherries and chocolate.

Dawn broke at around half past six. In the mountains to the north we caught a glimpse of something flashing; a massive thunderstorm was about to break. Soon we also heard the thunderclaps, and the number of seconds between flashes of lightning and thunderclaps indicated that the storm was just over five kilometres away, and coming towards us. We suddenly realised we were the highest points in the flat terrain, so we increased our pace to seek shelter as quickly as possible. Luckily only a few raindrops fell before we reached our destination.

In Mansilla de las Mulas we moved into the *refugio,* and slept through most of the morning. Sometime in the afternoon the storm really broke loose. The heavens opened wide, and flashes and thunderclaps followed in rapid succession. The rainfall was so heavy it almost became dangerous to be outdoors. A quick run across the backyard made me just as wet as if I had been hosed down, and the yard became so full of water that whirls of current were forming around the gully-hole. The overflowing water was streaming through the hall via the back door and out onto the street through the front door, it was just like a river. Those poor pilgrims who might be out on the plains in this weather would get thoroughly drenched!

In the Middle Ages the last stretch from Mansilla to León was described as being hostile, and it was not unusual for pilgrims to be robbed or murdered along this stretch. Today the Camino follows the main road, and the greatest danger is the busy and heavy traffic. Therefore we caught the bus through the rain for the last 15 kilometres to León.

THE ROAD FROM LEÓN
TO SANTIAGO

León is an ancient city. It was founded by the Roman legions which were encamped here, and acquired its name from them. The city was also the capital of Christian Spain, and is said to be one of Spain's most beautiful cities. It is busy, spacious and elegant with fountains on every *plaza*; a magnificent combination of old and new.

The old pilgrims' hostel of San Marcos was built as a convent in 1168 by the Knights of Saint James. The one hundred metre long façade is richly ornamented, and the scallop shell is commonly used as motif to show the connection with James and the Camino. The hostel has been turned into a luxurious *parador*, which is often described as the most beautiful hotel in the world. It still gives a small discount to pilgrims, to commemorate the hotel's original history.

James killing Moors on Hostal de San Marcos in León.

We indulged ourselves with a rest-day in León, and moved into a simple double-room in a *pénsion* on one of the avenues. The pension was situated in a dark flat on the second floor. Señora was sitting in the kitchen checking on how much water we used in the shower. Hot water cost extra, and the squeaking floorboards made it impossible to sneak unnoticed into the bathroom.

After breakfast we visited the cathedral of Santa Maria de la Regla. The noble Gothic cathedral is often described as one of the most elegant buildings in Europe. The stained-glass windows, dating from the 14th century, fill the church with light in a variety of colours. The windows are best observed in the evening, when the light makes their colours stand out from the dark building.

James is found in several versions in the church. He stands in a niche behind the altar, and next to one of the outside portals. During the centuries the column beneath the statue has been stroked by innumerable pilgrims, who have asked for his blessing along the road towards Santiago.

The day's main objective was to find me some new boots. The boots I bought in Saint-Jean were a little too small, and I had experienced great problems with blisters and sore toes since crossing the Pyrenees. I would have to swallow my pride and buy myself a new pair. Most Spaniards probably have smaller feet then me, but in a small specialist shop I tried various models from Señora's wide range in size 12 before reaching a decision. I was hoping my foot-problems would soon be over.

Our clothes were taken to a dry-cleaner's, and we visited San Marcos for a coffee and a look around its museum. Films, and what was left of unnecessary luggage, were packed in boxes and sent off. Now the rucksacks were almost empty, we had managed to dispose of most of our worldly possessions.

It was Midsummer's Eve, and León was packed with people who were going to watch the parade and enjoy the evening, even though the fiesta of San Juan, Saint John, did not start until the weekend. We found ourselves a small downstairs-restaurant, and had an excellent meal accompanied by the noise of the crowd outside. Afterwards

Bronze scallop shells lead the pilgrims through León.

we came across a small street-band, complete with a donkey and a barrel of wine, and were invited along to taste the wine. Their standard-bearer had presumably had several tastings, for suddenly he was lying flat on the ground covered by the standard. The band turned around to carry him home.

We returned to the pension, but our retiring to bed was delayed by a fantastic firework display. The tropical heat made it difficult to sleep, and neither of us were really rested when our alarms rang in the morning. The thermometer outside showed 17°C when we left the pension just before seven. No wonder we could not sleep.

The road ahead crossed the final stretch of the Meseta, which now reminded me of the African Savannah. Intense heat and lack of wood resulted in the building of troglodyte houses. One dug a hole in the hillside and supported the walls with bricks made from mud and straw. The only parts visible above ground are the chimney and the entrance. The houses reminded me of the houses of the

◄ *The Cathedral of Santa Maria de la Regla in León.*

The last stretch of the Meseta is similar to the African Savannah.

Hobbits in the book The Lord of the Rings, even though the doors are rectangular and not round.

The gravelled track was wide and even, and Mark and I were discussing various subjects of no importance as we walked along. Allan was somewhere ahead, and we got a little confused when his boot-prints suddenly began pointing in the wrong direction. He had only been a little uncertain about the route, and had gone back to a way-mark to double-check.

An old bridge crosses the Órbigo river, and led us to the village of Hospital de Órbigo. The bridge is a couple of hundred metres long, and built across twenty stone arches. It was built in the 13th century, and protected by the knights of León. When they could not withstand the temptation, they used the narrow bridge for tournaments and jousting.

After seven weeks along the road it became necessary to increase our intake of calories. It is said that you lose an amount of weight similar to the weight you carry on your back along the Camino. I had lost 8 kilograms and Mark 10, and neither of us were exactly overweight when we set off. The weight-loss was beginning to show, since we had burnt off our protecting layer of fat. Through my skin I could feel bones I had never felt before. The rucksack was feeling harder against my back, and the shock absorbing layer under my feet had almost entirely disappeared.

Our bodies had also changed in other ways. They had become stronger and leaner, our thighs and legs slimmer and more muscular and our waists narrower. The blisters were also healing, and my muscles and tendons were now hardly the cause of any trouble. This format could certainly be recommended for those wishing to diet; eat and drink whatever you like, as long as you make sure you walk a little in-between meals.

The physical strain was all-embracing, and the heat was draining off our energy. We had to make sure to maintain a physical and mental balance, to have enough strength to complete the journey and to appreciate the adventures yet to come. Food is an important source of energy, and soup is a good way of maintaining the liquid balance and prevent dehydration. The speciality caldo gallego; Galician meat and vegetable stock, is served in most restaurants, and is a tasty and nutritious food for pilgrims.

We had become accustomed to the daily stretches ranging from 25 to 35 kilometres, and after a rest-day our legs were itching to start walking again. Some days I even caught myself wondering if I was still carrying my ruck-sack. It felt very light, although still weighing around 25 kilograms.

My new boots were comfortable, and my big toes now had plenty of room. The boots had to be broken in, and when we arrived in Astorga after a short and uneventful walk, we agreed to stay until the following day. I would use the opportunity to gather my strength and update my journal, and when we had visited the Gothic cathedral and Antonio Gaudi's Art Nouveau Bishop's Palace I decided to find a peaceful spot in the park to have some time on my own.

Suddenly I recognised two people on the outskirts of the park; Serena and Richard! They had arrived in León that morning, but the city was so packed with people coming to the fiesta that they had caught the train to Astorga instead. I showed them the way to the refugio, where Mark and Allan were just as surprised to see them again. They told us about what was happening along the route behind us. Curtis was still walking, but they had not heard anything about Lala. Serena, Richard and Allan were joining us along the rest of the road to Santiago.

I took my journal to a table in the outdoor café in the park, and managed to complete my writing before wind, rain and thunder forced me indoors. My energy was returning, and I felt ready for a new stretch tomorrow.

In the evening the five of us went to a restaurant I had found during my wanderings around Astorga. The waiter came over as soon as we were inside the door, and I asked for «una mesa para cinco personas, por favor». The facial expressions of the other four showed they were impressed by my command of Spanish. The use of a language does not have to be perfect to be understood by other people. It is more important that the knowledge of the language covers the need to understand and be understood. To communicate in Spanish I sometimes just added an -o to Norwegian or English words, and slightly changed the structure of the sentence. A phrase like «contact lenses» thus became lenses contactico in my version, while lentas de contacto is correct, but it was close enough for the Spaniards to understand what I meant. In

The entrance to the Cathedral of Astorga.

Storks nesting in the Bishop's Palace.

Modern angel in Astorga.

addition I «Spaniardised» several English words. «Civilisation» became *civilización*, and although I could not form complete sentences, it was still possible to keep the conversation going by using gestures and body language. *Donde esta;* where is, was one of the most useful expressions to know when asking for directions.

The Bishop's Palace in Astorga.

The road westwards from Astorga goes through a broken terrain, with trees and bushes and mountain ridges in the horizon. We had reached the Maragatería, one of the wildest and most beautiful areas along the route. The climate here can be extremely cold, even in the summer.

The Rabanal Pass leads up to Rabanal del Camino, the last inhabited village before we crossed the Irago mountains. Here voluntary members of the English Jacobean organisation The Confraternity of Saint James run a pilgrim hostel. Refugio Gaucelmo is open to walkers, cyclists and

The Maragatería is one of the wildest areas along the pilgrim road.

Cruz de Hierro marks the highest point on the Camino.

pilgrims on horseback. The hostel opened in 1991, and has room for 30 pilgrims. By the end of 1995 more than 20,000 pilgrims had spent a night here. Of these only another four were Norwegians, the same number as from Uruguay.

Now in June the hostel was run by two middle-aged English ladies. They received us with generous hospitality, and showed us to our quarters after we had signed the visitors' book. The hostel is of high standard, modern and spacious, and run in the English style. Tea and coffee were served continuously, and I am certain it would be possible to sit in front of the fireplace reading The Times if we wanted to. My English travelling companions expected a visit to a small piece of British territory in the middle of the wilderness to be like coming home, and with the warm reception we received every one of us was feeling at home.

The hierarchic order amongst pilgrims is very strong. Walkers have the highest status, then cyclists and those on horseback. Motorists and coach passengers are at the bottom end of the hierarchy. A proper pilgrim stays overnight in monasteries and refugios. Fondas and pensiónes are acceptable, but staying in paradores is almost equivalent to heresy, and is quite unthinkable.

From Rabanal, the road continues uphill to the summit of Monte Irago. We passed the abandoned mountain village of Foncebadón, where wild dogs have taken control. They are said to be aggressive and ferocious, and we were advised to bring a long staff and have some pebbles ready in case the dogs came too close. When we walked past, they were dozing in the sun between the ruins. They hardly batted an eyelid, and did not give the slightest hint of being interested in passing pilgrims.

Cruz de Hierro marks the highest point on the Camino, 1504 metres above the sea. The point itself is marked by a high cross on top of a stone mound. Pilgrims crossing the pass are supposed to add a stone to the mound. Since the vicinity around the cross is almost free of stones, we brought some with us from further down the path to be able to follow the tradition. On the other side of the pass we descended steeply along heather-clad mountain sides until we stopped for the night in Molinaseca, 595 metres above the sea.

I had experienced stomach problems for a couple of days, and the small quantity of nourishment I managed to take in literally ran through the system. I felt fairly faint and weak, and although I still walked the planned stretches, I walked slowly and without much enthusiasm.

When I awoke in the refugio in Molinaseca my condition had reached its peak. Diagnosis: Acute diarrhoea! I swallowed two Imodium tablets, and tried to cool down with a cold shower. I packed my rucksack, and it felt as though everything was in order. I had to force down some breakfast to increase my level of energy, but was feeling very weak.

We set off at the usual time, and the 8 kilometres to Ponferrada were easily covered. The town looks like an unstructured heap of modern, inhospitable buildings from a distance, and the impression was not much improved when we walked into town.

In Ponferrada we met Serena and Richard again. Serena was also having problems with her stomach, which immediately made me feel a little better. We stopped in a bar to drink some lemonade. I fell into a heavy sleep by the table, and became almost impossible to wake. The thermometer was showing 21°C, although it was not yet ten o'clock, and the heat was causing my condition to get worse. Mark suggested we two «patients» should catch a bus the 19 kilometres to Villafranca del Bierzo. Under the circumstances this was probably the best solution. We made our way to the bus station, found the right service and bought our tickets. While the other two continued on foot, Serena and I longed for the bus to depart.

Villafranca was founded by French pilgrims sometime in the 13th century. It is a small town with several churches, and the town has always been a place for sick pilgrims. By the bridge Puente del Perdón pilgrims who were too sick to carry on to Santiago were granted absolution. I sincerely hoped our pilgrimage would not end in a similar way.

The road to the refugio was signposted from the bus stop, so we found our way with ease. What a refugio! It resembled a combination between a Bedouin tent and a hippie camp, and was made up of a steel construction covered with several layers of tarpaulin. A primitive irrigation system made sure that it did not get too hot under the canvas roof. The interior consisted of an earthen floor,

Thunderstorm over Galicia.

wooden tables and benches made from rustic beams and bricks. The hostel was built around the bar in the refectory. It was close to ten metres long, and seemed to contain everything we might possibly have wanted. Plans exist for a new hostel in Villafranca. It will surely be of a higher standard, but lacking in character. This place was perfect, with plenty of room.

The *refugio* is run by the Jato family, and we explained to Señora about our stomach problems when we arrived. She believed we might have drunk from a contaminated fountain near León, and made a mixture of water, sugar, salt, lemon and carbonated water before she ordered us to bed. The mixture was not exactly tasty, but after a few hours' sleep it seemed to be working.

Señor Jesús Jato has the reputation of being a healer, and several pilgrims asked him to heal their major and minor physical problems. I was willing to give it a try. He agreed to try and cure my stomach, and began washing his hands in cider before starting the treatment.

I stood straight up with my eyes closed, and felt him following the contour of my shoulders and arms downwards, continuing down my legs. Then he quickly touched my big toe. I felt his hands cold and cooling against my forehead, and warm against my stomach. It seemed to be working slightly, mainly due to the change of temperature where he placed his hands. The following day, however, proved that my condition had resisted Señor Jato's efforts…

In the evening we were invited to a *fiesta del fuerro;* a fire-water party. We gathered along the tables in the refectory together with a group of students from Andalucia, and when the lights were dimmed the ceremony began. Señor Jato poured spirit from a jar into a large iron saucepan, and ignited the liquid. While it burned he stirred it with a large ladle, and chanted a number of incantations. These were prayers to the positive spirits to stand us by, and warnings to the evil powers to stay away. The ritual is supposedly based on the old ceremonies held by the Celtic Druids. After each phrase a lengthy howl rose from the audience.

When the brew was ready the light was switched on, and glasses containing a bronze-coloured liquid smelling strongly of alcohol passed around. The potent brew was supposed to cleanse our minds, so we could sleep with a clean conscience. If it is true that good medicine is supposed to have a foul taste, there was no danger of us falling ill in the near future.

The path climbs uphill along wooded hillsides and green hedges towards O Cebreiro. The border to the region of Galicia is crossed along the way. From the border there are placed marker stones for every five hundredth metre. The stones show the remaining distance to Santiago, now we were only 152,5 kilometres from our goal!

O Cebreiro, the village in the clouds, is located near the summit of the Alto do Poio pass, 1300 metres above sea level. Here the warm and dry Meseta air meets the cold and humid Atlantic climate, and the luxuriant soil owes its character to this humid coastal climate. This time of the year it was normal to experience thunderstorms in the afternoon.

The need for shelters for pilgrims has always been great in these desolate mountain areas. The first hostel was built here as early as year 836, and was run by various monastic orders until the pilgrim traffic discontinued in the 19th century. The Gallegan authorities have built several modern *refugios* along the road over the past few years. The *refugio* in O Cebreiro is one of the largest, with room for 80 pilgrims.

The village itself consists of a group of houses with dry-stone walls. The oldest buildings are round with thatched roofs. In Gallego, the language spoken in Galicia, they are called *pallozas*. They are said to be built in the same way as Spanish dwellings built in pre-Roman times. Today the village is regarded as a cultural monument. Although modern tourism has left its mark here, much of the original atmosphere has been kept.

The village church was built in the 10th century. It became widely known along the pilgrim roads due to a miracle which happened early in the 14th century. A shepherd from one of the nearby hamlets used to attend evening mass. On a dark winter's night a blizzard was howling outside the church walls, but the old shepherd came to church as always. The priest was not as strong a believer, and hinted that only a fool would be coming to church to receive some bread and wine on such a night. Suddenly there was a clap of thunder, and the communion bread and wine were transformed into proper flesh and blood. The priest probably became a stronger believer afterwards.

The chalice was reputed to be the Holy Grail, the cup Jesus used when he instigated the communion. The Grail was also used to collect some of his blood after his crucifixion, and according to the legend it still contains a few drops of Jesus' blood. During the Crusades, one of the objectives of the Knights Templar was to find the Grail, but none of them ever succeeded in their task.

The bread and the wine were placed in a shrine given to the church by Queen Isabella. She tried to have the relics moved, but the mules planned for their transport refused to move. This was seen as a heavenly sign, and the shrine still remains in the church of O Cebreiro. The remains of the bread and the wine are still kept in the shrine. You can imagine what they might look like after nearly 700 years' storage.

The sun had been shining from a deep-blue sky all day, but in the afternoon a massive thunderstorm broke. Fortunately we were indoors, and for a while the sky was filled with flashes, and the thunderclaps were so heavy and long-drawn that it was impossible to tell one from the other. Then it began hailing. The hailstones were the size of peas, and the wind whipped them against the roof and windows so hard that it became almost impossible to keep a conversation going. The hail-showers changed into heavy rain after a while. Everywhere was overflowing; the soil was running in rapid, brown torrents down the stairs outside the hostel, and the village street had been turned into a brook by the heavy rainfall. Several times lightning struck nearby, and we saw treetops get splintered and branches broken off by its force. While we were standing looking curiously through the window, a lightning bolt struck a treetop only 20 metres away, and a massive bang shook the whole house; the hostel had been struck. Luckily the lightning-conductor led it into the ground before it did any damage, but the electricity was gone.

The storm began to ease after a couple of hours. According to the local population storms like this were not uncommon, and the following week we encountered rain and thunder every afternoon. It usually started at around five, and lasted for a couple of hours.

From the Alto do Poio pass, the road descends along steep hillsides covered in ferns, bushes, trees, lilies and other flowers. We had now crossed our last great mountain range, and down in the lowlands we would be following country roads, cart tracks and paths over the last 140 kilometres to Santiago.

The walking was easy. The countryside reminded me of the inner valleys of Southern Norway, it was luxuriant and green with large hedges and colourful verges. The countryside was often shrouded in a veil of fog in the mornings, but it normally lifted off before midday. June was coming to an end, and the daily stretches were becoming shorter and shorter. Now we were so close to our goal that we could allow ourselves to take it easier. We were not in any hurry, and wanted to enjoy the adventures in full measure. Thus we took time to stop where we wanted, and had plenty of chocolate- and coffee-stops during the day.

The closer we got to Santiago, the more pilgrims we met. It was getting rather crowded in the hostels, and since most of us were walking the same stretches we often engaged in lively chatter with old acquaintances.

The unity between the pilgrims was amazing. Every-

Top: *Galicia is clearly influenced by the humid Atlantic climate.* Bottom: *Cattle is an important source of income in rural parts of Galicia.*

Top: *99 kilometres left to the Apostle's grave!* Bottom: *Galician pilgrim fountain.*

body walking to Santiago was on the same road, regardless of social background or reason for doing the walk. We went through some of the same experiences, shared the hardship and the pleasant adventures with each other, and exchanged experiences from the road behind us and information about the road ahead.

Portomarin is an old town built in a new place. The building of a dam and a water reservoir across the Miño river made it necessary to move the town in 1962. The chief buildings were marked and dismantled stone by stone, and rebuilt on dry land higher up the hillside. The old pilgrim route disappeares into the water on both sides of the valley. When the water level is low, the ruins of the original town protrude above the masses of water. It struck me what extensive alterations man's attempts to control nature have led to. The valley with fields and houses had completely vanished, and where there used to be a living town there is now only water.

We arrived in Portomarin via a long bridge across the water reservoir, and found the *refugio* in the old school with ease. Here there was the luxury of a washing machine, and we used the opportunity to get our clothes properly washed. The daily thunderstorm set in at its usual time, just when we were about to put our washing out to dry. We found a covered yard where we could stretch our clotheslines, and hoped for enough draught to dry off the worst humidity.

The *refugio* filled up during the afternoon and evening, and for the first time I met other Scandinavian pilgrims. Four middle-aged Swedes were spending three weeks on their journey from Saint-Jean to Santiago. They had chosen to walk only the best parts of the route, and caught a bus along the rest. Now they wanted to walk the final 100 kilometres required to receive the Compostela in the cathedral. The Swedes had not met other Scandinavians along the route either, and asked if they could photograph the Norwegian pilgrim for their family album. I allowed myself to be persuaded.

The road from Portomarin follows cart tracks between green fields and meadows. The sun was shining from an almost cloudless sky, and the countryside was again similar to Dartmoor in Southern England. It was almost as if Plymouth was just around the bend, and that we could pop into our good friend Arezoo's house for tea.

Despite the tiredness after the completed stretches, we had enough energy left in the afternoons to look around. I was feeling pleasantly relaxed, and did not feel the restless need to walk on. The relaxing feeling in the evening was a bliss, and my blood pressure was lower than it had been for a long time.

The population of Galicia is shy and reticent compared to other Spaniards. The Gallegans are often described as superstitious, old-fashioned and generally suspicious of foreigners. It was more difficult to get chatting to local people along this part of the route. Often they were «occupied» with something, and had their backs towards us when we walked by, even if they could not have avoided noticing us. Our *buenos diaz* was answered in a hesitating voice, it lacked the enthusiasm and following conversation we were used to.

Over the last few nights we had stayed in packed *refugios*, and it seemed that most pilgrims were walking the same daily stretches as us. Most of them were going to stay in Palas de Rey, an uninteresting little town where the population is described as «unusually unhelpful and dismissive towards pilgrims», so we continued to Casanova, a tiny hamlet in the woods. We did not expect there to be a shop or bar in Casanova, so necessary provisions were bought before leaving Palas de Rey. Serena, Richard, Allan and Marcus, a young chemical engineer from Frankfurt, joined us when we continued at a rapid pace on the last four kilometres to our overnight stop.

In Casanova we stopped outside the only house we saw to ask for the key to the *refugio*. Señora led us to a larger building up the road after we had signed the pilgrim book in her garage. The dates in the book were not recent, and she was obviously happy to be having pilgrims staying again.

The *refugio* was of the same good standard we had grown used to in Galicia. Señora chatted as she showed us the facilities, and invited us down for supper. She brought us a full menu, and every one of us ticked off their choice. We were well settled before the daily rain set in.

◄ *Pilgrims walking through the eucalyptus forests of Galicia.*

After a pleasant siesta, and repeated attempts to update our journals, we walked the 50 metres down to Señora's house. She introduced herself as Carmen, and showed us into the garage where she had laid a long table with a white tablecloth and burning candles. We were expecting everyone to be served their choice from the menu, and were a little startled when we realised that Carmen was expecting everyone to eat all of the ordered dishes!

The food was excellent. We enjoyed home-made soup, tomato salad, roasted chicken, fish and fried green peppers. For dessert we were served an interesting mixture of white cheese and *membrillo*; quince marmalade. Home-made wine was served with the meal, and Carmen laced the coffee with *agua ardiente*; a clear spirit made from pressed grapes. All the time Carmen bustled in and out of the garage to make sure everything was in order, and she did her share to ensure we had a wonderful meal in simple surroundings. The cost of the meal was unreasonably low. A night out in Carmen's garage cost about the same as a pint in Norway.

The following morning we were back in the garage, where we enjoyed breakfast with coffee and *magdalenas*; small soft cakes. Carmen was again the perfect hostess, and we would not mind spending a few extra days in her company.

The weather was not the best this Sunday morning. Low cloud with a light drizzle was hanging over the countryside. The temperature and rain was pleasant, but after having walked for a while it became necessary to put on our raincoats. All six of us were walking together for most of the day, but Mark and I, with our long legs, were slightly in front of the others.

In Melide, Sunday is the fiesta and market day, and the town was crowded with old people in a festive mood. On the pavement a lady was washing something in a tub; she was cleaning octopus! We had reached a *pulperia*; an octopus restaurant. Near to the tub a fire was lit underneath a drum, and here the octopus was cooked before being sliced and served inside the restaurant. The restaurant is built in an old warehouse. The decor of the place was rustic, with dim lighting, long tables, wooden benches and sawdust on the floor. People of all ages, dressed in black, were gathering along the tables, and

Squid cooking in Melide.

there was a sense of expectation in the air; the octopus was about to be served. Wooden plates with octopus were carried in and put onto the tables, and we used toothpicks to help ourselves. Wine was served in brown clay bowls, and large baskets filled with bread were put at each end of the table. This was Spanish Sunday breakfast at its best!

Soon we were back on the green path underneath scented eucalyptus trees and walking along lush meadows. The theory that there was always a climb after we had eaten was still holding good. The rain was staying away, even if the humidity was high. The path was fairly washed out, it had evidently been raining heavily here lately. The last part of the stretch to the *refugio* in Ribadiso de Baixo went through relatively even terrain.

We had got two more days of walking before our pilgrimage was completed. I was not really ready to arrive in Santiago yet, but had to realise the journey would soon be over. It would be strange to return to civilisation and reality again, hopefully as a renewed and somehow better human being. Santiago was a symbol of a new beginning for the medieval pilgrims. Would the city be the same for us?

Along the last stretch towards Santiago we kept a good pace along gravelled tracks, through eucalyptus forests and past farmsteads. Gallegan farms are not as mechanised as farms in the rest of Europe. Horses and oxen are still used as draught animals, and the meadows are cut with scythes. Often we saw black clad women, with straw hats protecting them from the sun, doing the heaviest labour. They herd the cattle and work in the cornfields, while the men are occupied elsewhere. The people here are evidently marked by the sun and the wind.

The villages we passed through were not attractive, and we only stopped to eat or buy provisions. We crossed the main road several times, and I could appreciate how the moose must feel when approaching a motor road. It was not us crossing their track, but the cars crossing ours.

The medieval pilgrims' last stop before Santiago was by the river Lavacolla. Here they had a bath so as to be clean when arriving in the City of the Apostle. Santiago Airport is today situated by the river, and the water is not so clean that we would become noticeably cleaner. Moreover, the standard of hygiene along the road has improved considerably over the past thousand years, so we did not have the same need for a thorough cleansing as did our predecessors.

After the bath the pilgrims hurried to the top of Monte del Gozo; Mount Joy, to view the three spires on the cathedral in Santiago for the first time. The first person to reach the summit was nicknamed Roy; King, and could use this title as a part of his surname afterwards.

We stopped in San Marcos to walk the final five kilometres to Santiago early the following morning. Prior to the Pope's visit in 1989, the green hillside was levelled to receive the large crowd of followers. Today San Marcos is a large complex with an amphitheatre and restaurants, and can accommodate up to 2,900 people. The living-area looks like a combination of a holiday camp and military barracks. One of the barracks is reserved for pilgrims. On the top of the hill stands a modern and unfascinating pilgrim monument, and the complete complex has more in common with areas for cheap mass-tourism than the end of a walking route with a history spanning over a thousand years. The Finnish lady at reception allocated us to an eight-man room, and we slept well this last night along the pilgrim road.

SANTIAGO DE COMPOSTELA, THE CITY OF THE APOSTLE

On our last day as pilgrims there was a morning mist lying densely over the terrain. The visibility was restricted, so we cancelled our scheduled climb to the top of Monte del Gozo. Instead our six-man group started on the final five kilometres towards the cathedral in Santiago.

The outskirts of the city are similar to most cities', with traffic arteries, business premises, blocks of flats and unexciting architecture. Slowly we approached the old town, and caught sight of the spires of the cathedral as we approached the Puerta del Camino, the old city gate reserved for pilgrims. The gate itself has been removed, and a small sign is all that marks the spot where it once stood.

Narrow streets led us towards the cathedral. Here they are supposed to have walked; Emperor Charlemagne, Bishop Gottschalk, Francis of Assisi and other personalities from medieval history. I was expecting the very last stretch to be a somewhat emotional experience, but did not feel any strong emotions about having reached our goal. Perhaps it was a confusing combination of relief at having arrived at our destination, and a lack of understanding of this being the final goal?

We walked across the Plaza del Obradoiro to take a closer look at the cathedral. James figures as a pilgrim in several versions on the Baroque façade, with cloak, hat and scallop shell. On top of the city hall across the square he proceeds as Santiago Matamoros on horseback with his sword aloft. This is undoubtedly the City of the Apostle.

The pilgrim traffic made Santiago into a prosperous and well-kept city. The old town with its elegant ecclesiastical buildings, its narrow streets, its covered arcades and its *plazas* is described as a Baroque masterpiece. It was named by UNESCO as a «Universal Heritage of Humanity» in 1985.

The Cathedral of Santiago de Compostela.

≺ *The cathedral complex in Santiago de Compostela.*

The cathedral seen from the Plaza del Obradoiro.

Top: *The Battle of Clavijo on top of the town hall in Santiago.* Bottom: *James above the Puerta Santa, the holy door only open during Holy Years.*

The city's 80,000 inhabitants claim that those who have not experienced the rain in Santiago have not been to Santiago. They say the loveliness of their city only emerges in the rain. That might be so, since the buildings are mainly built from granite, which tends to come to life when wet, but it might also be a part of their marketing campaign to draw more visitors. The local climate is fairly similar to the humid West-Country climate of England, and it rains an average 120 days a year.

In the Tourist Office we were fitted out with maps and information about sights and overnight accommodation. The certificate proving we had completed our pilgrimage, the Compostela, is granted by the cathedral pilgrim secretariat when a valid pilgrim's record is presented. We lined up together with an international congregation of pilgrims. The pilgrim's records, with all the stamps we had collected along the road from Le Puy, were presented, and we had to answer a few questions about our journey before we were properly registered in the large pilgrims' registry. Then our names were written in Latin on the certificates. I was named Dominum Canutum Helgum, which supposedly means Saint Canute the Holy, and was now convinced I have a holy name. Mark was not visibly impressed.

The present cathedral was begun around the year 1073 and completed in the 18th century. Hidden behind the richly ornamented façade is a simpler Romanesque architecture. The cross-shaped nave has been altered and extended so many times during the centuries that the enormous cathedral complex has acquired an almost quadratic shape.

The building of the cathedral was funded through a very controversial tax. All parts of Spain liberated from the Moors with the aid of James had to pay a special tax to the cathedral. This tax was only abolished during the last century. In 1598 the cathedral was almost destroyed by Sir Francis Drake, who set out with a 14,000 strong army to destroy this «stronghold of pernicious superstition», as he put it. Sir Frances was probably not a strong believer of the Jacobean legend.

Saint James on the central arch of the Portico de la Gloria.

The pilgrims' first destination is the main portal Portico de la Gloria; the Portal of Glory. This massive sculptural complex is considered a monument to medieval sculpture. The portal is composed of three arches with carved sculptures. At the top of the central marble arch stands Saint James, dressed as a pilgrim. By tradition our pilgrimage was completed when we placed our right hand fingers between the twisted stems of the Tree of Jesse; Christ's family tree, which is carved into the central pillar. The incised mark of four fingers and a thumb is a legacy from the pilgrimages, made by millions of pilgrims throughout the centuries. With the hand in place I asked for the blessing of the Apostle.

The next ritual was to embrace the Capilla Mayor, a silver statue of the Apostle dating from sometime before the 12th century. Pilgrims are allowed to climb the stairs behind the high altar to embrace the richly deco-

≺ View of the cathedral façade towards Plaza del Obradoiro.

The northern façade of Santiago Cathedral.

The horse fountain on the Plaza de las Platerías outside the cathedral.

rated statue from behind and place their hats on the Apostle's head. This is the climax of the journey for many pilgrims.

Every day a special pilgrims' mass is celebrated in the cathedral, and we should attend this mass on the day we had received our Compostelas. Towards the end of the

The old parts of Santiago.

service all pilgrims receive a special blessing for having made the pilgrimage to the grave of the Apostle, and a summary of the day's register of pilgrims and their nationalities is read out from the pulpit. «Uno peregrino Noruego», said the priest, a Norwegian pilgrim had been registered.

Thereafter the priest started making preparations for the communion. We could not take communion since we are not Catholics, but could receive the church's blessing insted. When the other pilgrims rose to walk towards the

high altar, we followed suit. We were walking up in two rows, and the priest was handing out the wafers, either by placing it in the mouth or the hands of each person. By having completed the pilgrimage we are granted absolution from half our time in purgatory, which might prove useful sometime in the future.

At special masses the 2.5 metre high censer *botafumeiro* is swung back and forth above the high altar. It travels the complete length of the transept. The incense was a necessity in the Middle Ages, when the church was often packed with pilgrims and personal hygiene was of another standard than today. It takes eight men to set the 80 kilogram silver censer in motion, using an ingenious block and tackle arrangement. The censer reaches a high velocity, and swings like a pendulum with sparks flying over the heads of the congregation. I could not help wondering what might happen if the rope snapped, but con-

∧ The pilgrim El Quiote and the donkey Filipa have completed yet another pilgrimage.

⋎ Modern relics in the City of the Apostle.

soled myself by remembering that this had supposedly happened only twice since the censer was introduced in the 15th century. While the censer was swinging back and forth, the cathedral was filled with the pleasant smell of incense. Chords from Bach's Toccata in D minor were flowing from the church organ, and the magic atmosphere was sending shivers down my spine. This was one of the highlights of the journey, and a worthy conclusion to our pilgrimage. When the time came to stop the censer, one of the men dressed in burgundy gripped onto it and made a pirouette-like movement to stop it.

The main goal for the journey was to see the relics of Saint James. They were hidden when the English fleet attacked Galicia sometime in the 18th century, and were not rediscovered until 1879. Now they are kept in a richly decorated silver coffer behind iron bars in the crypt underneath the high altar. A constant queue of pilgrims and tourists move through the crypt from early morning until late in the evening.

According to tradition, pilgrims and other believers kneel before a carved little statue of Maestro Mateo, the master carver, before leaving the cathedral. I lowered my head, and let my forehead touch the master's head. Then I would acquire some of the old master's talent and wisdom, or so it is said.

Outside the cathedral we bade farewell to Marcus, who was going to visit friends in Orense further south. Along the Camino he had found answers to many questions, and had decided to become a priest when he returned to Frankfurt. He is a strong-willed young man, who will try to modernise some of the attitudes of the Catholic church. I wish him good luck!

The Compostela entitles pilgrims to free meals for up to three days in the canteen in the Hostal de los Reyes Catolicos, which is set diagonally across the Plaza del Obradoiro from the cathedral. The Catholic Monarchs, Ferdinand and Isabella, founded this hostel in 1492, the year Columbus rediscovered America. Like most of the old hostels it has been turned into a parador, but pilgrims are invited to dine here to keep the old tradition alive.

≺ *The entrance to the Hostal de Los Reyes Catolicos.*

Λ *King David on the Platerías façade of the cathedral.*

Capilla de las Animas.

We had to find more reasonably priced overnight accommodation, and moved into a simpler *hostal* by the cathedral. During the first night we discovered why the room was so reasonable; the cathedral bells rang several times each hour! They struck once fifteen minutes past the hour, twice after thirty minutes, three times after forty-five minutes and four times on the hour. On top of this, a separate bell struck the total hours past midnight or midday. This added up to a considerable number of chimes during the night, and made a good night's sleep almost impossible!

Our first complete day in Santiago was spent exploring the city. After lunch Mark and I visited the Hostal de los Reyes Catolicos for a cup of hot chocolate and a slice of cake, an experience highly recommended by one of our guidebooks. Two cups of delicious, creamy chocolate and two generous slices of cake cost almost as much as a full dinner for two, but after ten weeks along the road we deserved a little luxury.

On our way out through the hotel lounge I recognised a dialect from Bergen, Norway. I could not restrain myself from revealing my country of origin, and stopped for a chat. It proved to be a Norwegian party of fourteen people, the first Norwegians I had encountered since leaving for Paris. They had walked the final 100 kilometres of the pilgrim road, but had stayed in hotels and not in *refugios*. Most of their luggage had been transported by coach, which to us pilgrims seemed like cheating. They found it a little impressive that we had walked from Le Puy, and asked a range of questions about our journey and our experiences. We discovered we had common acquaintances, and one of the men had attended a special fu-

The façade of the monastery of San Martín Pinario. ➤

View over Santiago de Compostela.
Top: *James killing Moors in Santiago.* Bottom: *Detail from the horse fountain on the Plaza de las Platerías.*

Top: *View from our hotel room towards the bells of Santiago Cathedral.*
Bottom: *Rainy street in Santiago.*

«Those who haven't experienced the rain in Santiago haven't been to Santiago».

The road leading to Finisterre.

Fishing boats in the harbour of Finisterre.

neral I was telling Mark about when we were crossing the Pyrenees. What a small world!

The Plaza del Obradoiro proved to be the perfect meeting point. Every day we met other pilgrims there. Our constantly smiling Spanish friend, Amigo, arrived a few days after us. He was pleased to see us, and was chatting away as usual. He knew we only understood a few of his words, but we answered as well as we possibly could. We never met Lala again.

After three days in Santiago the body was itching to walk on. We continued to Cape Finisterre to complete our walk on the cliffs by the ocean, and spent three days covering the 85 kilometres to get there.

Finisterre was the western edge of the known world until Columbus made it necessary to redesign the maps of the world. A stone cross marks this to be the end of the road from Place du Plot in Le Puy.

Dark cliffs fall steeply into the breakers beneath the lighthouse on the cape. While the sun was setting over the surface of the ocean, five exhausted wanderers sat on the edge of the cliffs looking towards the ocean and the light. We drank white wine from a bottle, and toasted our hopes for the future. All the adventures, experiences, joys and blisters had made our pilgrimage into the journey of a lifetime. Before darkness came we turned our noses eastwards again, like so many other pilgrims before us.

Herru Sanctiagu	Lord Santiago,
Got Sanctiagu	good Santiago,
Eultreia, e suseia	onwards, upwards,
Deus, adjuva nos.	and may God help us.

Pilgrims hymn from before the 12th century.

≺ *A stone cross marks the end of the road from Le Puy.*

AFTERMATH

The medieval pilgrims were ordinary people burning for a cause they believed in. As God's Travellers, they were to travel in simplicity and with gratitude. They were inviolate, and entitled to safe-conduct along the road. Anyone robbing or killing a pilgrim could expect to be condemned to the severest punishment.

As walkers, the pilgrims carried with them their culture and their history, and they exchanged experiences, thoughts and ideas along the way. The pilgrim roads therefore laid the foundation for more than a thousand years of cultural and historical movement through Europe. Until the Renaissance religion was the sole source of inspiration for all great works of art. All creativity, wealth and technical inventions were used in creating religious art and architecture. The great cathedrals were built as symbols of worship, and as symbols of how far humankind had developed under the protection of God. Along the pilgrim roads art and architecture were used to inspire the pilgrims and guide them to their goal. The roads did not only lead to Santiago, they also led to renewal and inspiration for those who followed them.

A modern pilgrimage is a journey out of time. It does not have to be based on the Christian faith. There are as many reasons to set out on such a journey as there are pilgrims. Today's pilgrims are often people standing at a crossroads in their lives. They need time to reflect upon the different possibilities before making their decision. Along the road there are few distractions, and travelling the route becomes more important than reaching the goal.

By undertaking a pilgrimage we were maintaining a tradition. As modern pilgrims we have gained great respect for those who walked before us. Their needs were simple, and we have learnt that less luggage gives us more freedom. The journey has undoubtedly changed our understanding of the world around us. Life is no longer the same struggle for survival as it was for our forefathers. Maybe our material abundance has led us to lose touch with the divinity within ourselves?

The story of James and his connection with Spain is based solely on the Jacobean legend. It emanates from a forged letter purporting to be written by Pope Leo III, but there is no historic proof that the story is true. The legend appeared when the church needed a gathering figure in the fight to expel the Moors from Europe. Galicia is Celtic country, and it is likely that the legend is based on a pre-Christian ritual which drew sun-worshippers to the shores of the immense Western Ocean.

Several critical Gallegans claim that the bones in the silver coffer in Santiago are not the remains of any apostle, but of Pricillian of Avilla, a bishop executed for heresy sometime in the 4th century. Regardless of who might be in the coffer, the legend of Saint James and the road to Santiago makes a fascinating story.

ITINERARY

30TH APRIL – 4TH JULY 1995

Day	Stretch	Distances in kilometres
1	Le Puy – Monistrol-d'Allier	27.5
2	Monistrol-d'Allier – Le Villeret d'Apchier	22.0
3	Le Villeret d'Apchier – La Roche	12.0
4	La Roche – Aumont-Aubrac	22.0
5	Aumont-Aubrac	0.0
6	Aumont-Aubrac – Nasbinals	0.0
7	Nasbinals – Saint-Chély-d'Aubrac	17.0
8	Saint-Chély-d'Aubrac – Espalion	22.0
9	Espalion – Estaing	11.0
10	Estaing – Golinhac	16.0
11	Golinhac – Conques	22.0
12	Conques – Livinhac-le-Haut	23.5
13	Livinhac-le-Haut – Figeac	24.5
14	Figeac – Béduer	12.5
15	Béduer – Cajarc	19.0
16	Cajarc – Vaylats	33.0
17	Vaylats – Cahors	25.0
18	Cahors	0.0
19	Cahors – Escayrac	27.0
20	Escayrac – Lauzerte	16.0
21	Lauzerte – Moissac	31.0
22	Moissac – Saint-Antoine	33.0
23	Saint-Antoine – Lectoure	28.0
24	Lectoure – Condom	30.0
25	Condom	0.0
26	Condom – Seviac	19.0
27	Seviac – Nogaro	35.0
28	Nogaro – Aire-sur-l'Adour	32.0
29	Aire-sur-l'Adour – Arsacq-Arraziguet	30.0
30	Arsacq-Arraziguet – Arthez-de-Béarn	26.5
31	Arthez-de-Béarn – Navarrenx	28.5
32	Navarrenx – Saint-Palais	30.0
33	Saint-Palais – Saint-Jean-Pied-de-Port	33.0
34	Saint-Jean-Pied-de-Port	0.0
35	Saint-Jean-Pied-de-Port – Roncesvalles	26.0
36	Roncesvalles – Larrasoaña	27.0

Day	Stretch	Distances in kilometres
37	Larrasoaña – Cizur Menor	20.0
38	Cizur Menor – Puente la Reina	22.0
39	Puente la Reina – Irache	26.0
40	Irache – Viana	35.0
41	Viana – Navarette	22.0
42	Navarette – Nájera	13.0
43	Nájera – Santo Domingo de la Calzada	18.0
44	Santo Domingo – Villafranca	34.0
45	Villafranca Montes del Oca – Burgos	38.0
46	Burgos	0.0
47	Burgos – Hornillos	19.0
48	Hornillos – Itero de la Vega	29.0
49	Itero de la Vega – Villalcázar de Sirga	24.0
50	Villalcázar de Sirga – Sahagún	46.0
51	Sahagún	0.0
52	Sahagún – León	37.0
53	León	0.0
54	León – Hospital del Orbigo	36.0
55	Hospital del Orbigo – Astorga	15.0
56	Astorgas – Rabanal del Camino	20.0
57	Rabanal del Camino – Molinaseca	25.0
58	Molinaseca – Villafranca del Bierzo	27.0
59	Villafranca del Bierzo – O Cebreiro	28.0
60	O Cebreiro – Triacastela	21.0
61	Triacastela – Barbadelo	23.0
62	Barbadelo – Portomarin	17.0
63	Portomarin – Casanova	28.0
64	Casanova – Ribadiso de Baixo	20.0
65	Ribadiso de Baixo – San Marcos	36.0
66	San Marcos – Santiago de Compostela	5.0
67	Santiago de Compostela	0.0
68	Santiago de Compostela	0.0
69	Santiago de Compostela – Negreira	21.0
70	Negreira – Olveiroa	29.0
71	Olveiroa – Finisterre	34.0
	TOTAL DISTANCE	**1,529.0 kilometres**

EQUIPMENT

This is all we needed along the road:

BASIC EQUIPMENT:
rucksack with side-pockets
waterproof stuff sacks
first aid kit
tape and plaster against blisters
compass
map case
torch

CLOTHING:
light woollen socks, 2 pairs
heavy woollen socks, 2 pairs
underpants, 3 pairs
shorts
light long trousers, 1 pair
2 T-shirts, wool
fleece sweater for walking
fleece sweater spare
scarf
GoreTex jacket
GoreTex trousers
mountain boots
sandals

SLEEPING ACCESSORIES:
sleeping bag
silk liner
pillow

EATING UTENSILS:
water bottle
Swiss Army Knife
lock blade pocket knife
plastic mug
teaspoon
matches

TOILETRIES:
soap
towel
toothbrush
toothpaste
razor
nail file/scissors
toilet tissue

OTHER:
washing powder
clothes-pegs
nylon clothesline, 3-4 m
sewing kit
passport/money case
walking stick
reflector disc
sunglasses
E111 form
travel insurance card
camera gear

MAPS:
France:
Topo-Guides 613, 617 and 621
with maps in scale 1:50.000.

The Pyrenees:
Maps in scale 1:25.000.

Spain:
Map book in scale 1:50.000 in Navarra,
and Spanish guidebook with hand-drawn
maps. Topographical maps are rarely up-
dated or accurate.

BIBLIOGRAPHY

Dante Alighieri, *Nyt Liv: La Vita Nuova*, transl. Johannes Dam, Munksgaard, København 1965

Kate Baillie & Tim Salmon, *The Rough Guide to France*, Rough Guides Ltd, London 1994

James Bentley, *The Way of Saint James*, Pavillion, London 1992

Hal Bishop, *The Way of Saint James: The GR 65*, Cicerone Press, Milnthorpe, Cumbria 1989

Glyn Burgess (transl.), *The Song of Roland*, Penguin Books, England 1990

Catalán, Mora & Tamargo, *El Camino de Santiago a pie*, El Pais Aguilar, Madrid 1993

Marc Dubin, *Trekking in Spain*, Lonely Planet Publications, Australia 1990

Mark Ellingham & John Fisher, *The Rough Guide to Spain*, Rough Guide Ltd, London 1994

David Hugh Farmer, *The Oxford Dictionary of Saints*, Oxford University Press, Oxford 1992

Eivind Luthen, *På Pilegrimsferd*, Pilegrimsforlaget, Oslo 1995

Gobierno de Navarra, *The pilgrim route to Santiago; GR-65 Navarre*, Pamplona 1992

Robin Hanbury-Tenison, *Spanish Pilgrimage – A Canter to St James*, Arrow Books, London 1991

Phinella Henderson (editor), *A Pilgrim Anthology*, The Confraternity of Saint James, London 1994

James Hogart (transl.), *The Pilgrim's Guide*, The Confraternity of Saint James, London 1992

Erla Bergendahl Hohler, *Stavkirkeportalene og deres symbolikk*, article, Årbok til Foreningen for Norske Fortidsminnesmerkers bevaring, Oslo 1995

Iglesias & Perrín, *A Guide to Santiago Cathedral*, Edilesa, Spain 1994

Michael Jacobs, *The Road to Santiago de Compostela*, Penguin, London 1992

Manuel Chamoso Lamas, *Santiago de Compostela*, Silex, Spain 1982

Erik Lorange, *Historiske byer*, Universitetsforlaget, Oslo 1990

Millán Bravo Lozano, *A practical guide for pilgrims*, Editorial Everest S.A., Spain 1993

Donald Matthew, *Atlas of Medieval Europe*, Facts on File, New York 1992

William Melczer, *The Pilgrim's Guide to Santiago de Compostela*, Italica Press, New York 1993

Monasterio de Santa Maria la Real de Najera, *Souvenir Guide*, Editorial Escudo de Oro, Spain 1995

Edwin Mullins, *The Pilgrimage to Santiago*, Secker & Warburg, London 1974

Myers, Simmons, Pierce, *Santiago, saint of two worlds*, University of New Mexico Press 1991

Patricia Quaife (editor), *Pilgrim Guides to Spain – The 'Camino Francés' 1995*, The Confraternity of Saint James, London 1995

Alison Raju, *The Way of St James: Spain*, Cicerone Press, Milnthorpe, Cumbria 1994

Alison Raju, *Le Puy to the Pyrenees*, The Confraternity of Saint James, London 1995

Cartography by Dr. Elías Valiña Sampedro, *The Way of St James - The Pilgrimage Route to Santiago de Compostela*, Roger Lascelles, Brentford, Middlesex 1993

Bert Slader, *Pilgrims' Footsteps*, Quest Books, Northern Ireland 1989

Elías Valiña, *The Pilgrim's Guide to the Camino de Santiago*, Galaxia, Spain 1992

Jacobus de Voraigne, *The Golden Legend*, Arno Press, New York 1969